LEGENDS OF WARFARE

GROUND

Harley-Davidson WLA

The Main US Military Motorcycle of World War II

ROBERT S. KIM

SCHIFFER MILITARY

4880 Lower Valley Road   Atglen, PA 19310

Copyright © 2020 by Robert S. Kim

Library of Congress Control Number: 2019947353

Designed by Justin Watkinson
Type set in Impact/Minion Pro/Univers LT Std

ISBN: 978-0-7643-5924-8
Printed in China

Published by Schiffer Publishing, Ltd.
4880 Lower Valley Road
Atglen, PA 19310
Phone: (610) 593-1777; Fax: (610) 593-2002
E-mail: Info@schifferbooks.com
www.schifferbooks.com

For our complete selection of fine books on this and related subjects, please visit our website at www.schifferbooks.com. You may also write for a free catalog.

Schiffer Publishing's titles are available at special discounts for bulk purchases for sales promotions or premiums. Special editions, including personalized covers, corporate imprints, and excerpts, can be created in large quantities for special needs. For more information, contact the publisher.

We are always looking for people to write books on new and related subjects. If you have an idea for a book, please contact us at proposals@schifferbooks.com.

Contents

Introduction

The Harley-Davidson WLA, which served as the main US military motorcycle of the Second World War, is one of the iconic vehicles of that war and a significant milestone for the over 100-year-old Harley-Davidson Motor Company. Millions of people around the world have seen WLAs in wartime photographs or as restored survivors in museums and private collections, and WLAs are regularly featured in historical and fictional motion pictures set in the Second World War. Nevertheless, knowledge of how the US armed forces and other Allied armies used the WLA during the war is almost nonexistent. Little has been known about its actual military usage by the United States, and even less about its use by other Allied powers. The deficiency is especially pronounced for the Soviet Union, which used more WLAs than any other country—even the United States—and made them frontline combat vehicles in a way that no other country did.

The WLA went into production in 1940 to serve as the US Army's main motorcycle. Developed from the civilian model WL, the WLA initially went into wide usage with mechanized cavalry scouts and as general-purpose vehicles, and the US armed services acquired over 23,000 during the Second World War. WLAs were withdrawn from most US Army combat unit roles in 1942 after the introduction of the Jeep, and they all but disappeared from the official Army tables of organizations and equipment by 1944. They remained in frontline Army and Marine Corps service through the end of the war with couriers, military police, and others who found motorcycles to have unique advantages, moving them through the crowded vehicle traffic of modern battlefields.

A dozen other Allied countries also used the WLA and other Harley-Davidson and Indian motorcycles from the United States. Supplied to Allied powers under the Lend-Lease program or through direct sales, these tens of thousands of American motorcycles were part of the vast supply of American-made motor vehicles that kept Allied armies on wheels, giving them a significant advantage in mobility and logistical support over the largely horse-drawn German army.

The Soviet Union became the largest and most significant user of the WLA. The United States sent over 27,000 WLAs to the Soviet Union under the Lend-Lease program, and they became the Red Army's main motorcycle, the mainstay of key units of its armored forces. They served as the main combat vehicle of the Red Army's motorcycle battalions, the reconnaissance units of the tank armies that were the spearheads of the Red Army's offensive operations. These units built around American-made WLAs led the advance of the Red Army across Europe, from Stalingrad all the way to Berlin.

The story of the Harley-Davidson WLA began in America, expanded overseas during the course of the Second World War, and became a worldwide story by its end. This book will tell for the first time the full history of how American soldiers and Marines and other forces of the Allies used the WLA in Europe, North Africa, and Asia.

CHAPTER 1
Origins of the WLA

The legendary Harley-Davidson WLA emerged in 1940 from a modest civilian model. Harley-Davidson and its main domestic competitor, Indian, had sold motorcycles to the US armed forces since before the First World War, and more-sophisticated designs for military motorcycles had been introduced or were under development during the late 1930s, but the WLA came into existence for the Second World War on the basis of the Harley-Davidson WL, a model developed in 1937 from a design that dated back to 1929.

1929 Harley-Davidson DL.
Courtesy of dl45homepage.cm

In 1929, Harley-Davidson had introduced the Forty-Five, a midsized motorcycle by US standards of the time, with a 45-cubic-inch (750 cc) side-valve engine. It was substantially smaller and slower than the company's full-sized "big twin" Seventy-Four with its 74-cubic-inch (1,200 cc) side-valve engine. Available at first as the standard Model D as well as the more powerful DL (with a higher-compression engine) and the sidecar-equipped DS, then also as the sportier DLD in 1930, the Forty-Five competed against the Indian Scout 101, introduced in 1928.

Introduced during the year of the stock market crash that began the Great Depression, the Forty-Five sold in a collapsed market for motorcycles. Harley-Davidson sales fell from 20,946 in 1929 to 17,661 in 1930, then dropped steeply each year to 10,500 in 1931, 6,841 in 1932, and only 3,703 in 1933—1 percent of

Harley-Davidson production in 2006.[1] By 1939, sales recovered to 10,352, approximately 60 percent of 1929 levels. The Forty-Five served primarily as basic transportation in a grim and deprived era, with reliability and utility as its hallmarks rather than speed and sophistication.

Perhaps the ultimate Forty-Five was the Servi-Car, a three-wheeled utility vehicle that lasted from 1932 to 1974, twenty-two years after the discontinuation of the rest of Forty-Five line. Intended at first for use by garages and service stations as a means of picking up and delivering cars, the Servi-Car came equipped with a tow bar, allowing one employee to ride to a customer's house and pick up a car, towing the Servi-Car behind it, then return the car with the Servi-Car trailing behind it and ride the Servi-Car back. The Servi-Car also became popular with police departments and other

1932 Servi-Car brochure.
Courtesy of dl45homepage.com

1936 Servi-Car used as a self-propelled ice cream stand. *Courtesy of dl45homepage.com*

Close-up of a WLA engine, showing the aluminum cylinder heads introduced in 1939. *Courtesy of Wikimedia*

municipal users for use by parking-meter readers and other employees needing a small vehicle to move through city traffic. Some served as delivery vehicles for retail stores or in street vendor roles, such as self-propelled ice cream stands.[2]

The Forty-Five line continued to be powered by side-valve engines after Harley-Davidson and motorcycle manufacturers across the Atlantic introduced new overhead-valve designs that were more efficient and powerful. In 1936, Harley-Davidson introduced its Model 61E, nicknamed the "Knucklehead," an overhead-valve V-twin that gave Harley-Davidson a major advantage over its main rival, Indian, after three decades of seesaw competition. In Germany in the same year, BMW introduced its landmark R5, with an overhead-valve flat twin and the pioneering telescopic-fork front suspension that the company had debuted in 1935. A supercharged and streamlined overhead-valve BMW set a motorcycle speed record of 173.51 miles per hour (mph) in 1937, a record that would not be surpassed until 1951. In 1937, Triumph introduced its Speed Twin, with an overhead-valve parallel twin that gave Triumph a performance advantage over its competitors in the United Kingdom. These models established the signature engine designs that each company would continue to use into the twenty-first century.[3]

The most-important developments in the Forty-Five line before the Second World War were enhancements to its reliability and endurance, not its power and performance. After the successful introduction of the overhead-valve Knucklehead in 1936, Harley-Davidson considered producing an overhead-valve Forty-Five as well but decided against it.[4] The significant addition to the Forty-Five in 1937 was instead a less celebrated element of the Knucklehead design: a recirculating oil system, replacing the "total loss" system previously used. Whereas the total-loss system sent small amounts of oil on a one-way trip to friction points and then outside the engine to the ground, the recirculating system rapidly cycled oil into the engine at high pressure and then returned it to the oil tank. The recirculating system improved engine lubrication and

cooling and reduced oil consumption. Moreover, it eliminated a burden on the rider, removing the need to check the oil level and oil pump adjustment practically every day. With this modernization, Harley-Davidson redesignated the Forty-Five lineup as the Model W and Model WL.

A further major improvement to the Forty-Five came with the introduction of aluminum cylinder heads in the spring of 1939. First used on the WLD Special sports model, the aluminum heads kept the engine significantly cooler than the iron heads used in other Forty-Fives, thanks to the faster heat dissipation of aluminum and taller cooling fins with over 50 percent more surface area.[5] Iron heads, which were cheaper to produce, continued to be used on nonsports models. Originally designed for high-speed use on racetracks, the aluminum heads would soon keep military Forty-Fives running coolly and reliably while moving slowly in the harsh conditions of battlefields in Europe, Africa, and the Pacific.

Forty-Fives rolled out of the Harley-Davidson factory in the D series of 1929–1931, the R series of 1932–1936, and the W series of 1937–1951. Experience with real-world use over the course of a decade gave Harley-Davidson ample time and experience to discover and work out flaws in the design. By the outbreak of the Second World War, the Forty-Five was a thoroughly developed and proven design, with any inherent weaknesses affecting its reliability and durability continually addressed by ten years of annual improvements.

Development of the Forty-Five for military use began in 1939. The US Army had earlier used small numbers of the Forty-Five and the Seventy-Four but was dissatisfied with the suitability of these road-oriented machines for military use. Responding to a request from the Army in November 1938, Harley-Davidson built two experimental Forty-Fives and shipped them to Fort Knox, Kentucky, in August 1939. These two bikes were standard civilian models with a low-compression engine, the aluminum cylinder heads introduced a few months earlier on the WLD Special, cut-down front and rear fenders designed to trap less mud and debris,

Harley-Davidson motor trike, with the round oil bath air cleaner used on the WLA in 1941. *Courtesy of the National Archives*

Rear view of a Harley-Davidson motor trike. *Courtesy of the National Archives*

Indian 640, from War Department Technical Manual 10-515. *Courtesy of the US Army Military Police Corps Regimental Museum*

a skid plate to protect the engine, and olive paint.[6] Considered afterward to be prototypes of the WLA, these motorcycles entered Army tests that began in September 1939. During the following year, in response to an Army request for a vehicle to fill a military requirement for a motor trike, Harley-Davidson also submitted a three-wheeled version for testing at Fort Benning, Georgia.

Indian submitted the main competitor, a military version of its Scout model called the 640. The 640 had an engine reduced from 45 cubic inches (750 cc) to 30.5 cubic inches (500 cc), developed for military export sales in Europe, where engines with smaller displacements than in the United States were normal. The Army initially was interested in the 640 and requested that Harley-Davidson also build a 30.5-cubic-inch military motorcycle, but Harley-Davidson refused, declaring that the smaller displacement would result in a motorcycle underpowered for military use.[7] The Army agreed after further testing of the WLA and the 640, preferring the WLA with its original 750 cc displacement.

Whether US military motorcycles in the upcoming war would be based on existing machines or on new and more-advanced designs derived from foreign examples was in the balance from 1939 to 1941. While Harley-Davidson and Indian submitted modified versions of their existing commercial models, Delco—a division of General Motors not in the motorcycle business—sent newly designed motorcycles and motor trikes derived from BMW designs. Delco copied BMW's horizontally opposed twin-cylinder engine, shaft final drive, and telescopic front suspension. This design had significant advantages that were immediately apparent to Army testers: superior

cooling from having the cylinders projecting outward into the flow of air, instead of being tucked within the frame; a final drive system protected from mud and dirt, unlike the exposed chain drive used in Harley-Davidsons and Indians; and a smoother ride on rough roads and off-road from use of a hydraulically damped telescopic front fork, instead of old-fashioned undamped girder or springer forks. The Army expressed interest in acquiring motorcycles with these features, and Harley-Davidson and Indian each responded by developing new designs that departed completely from their traditional configurations.

Harley-Davidson met the Army's request by reverse engineering an existing BMW design, while Indian developed a new design from a clean sheet of paper. Harley-Davidson purchased a civilian model, BMW R71, a 750 cc side-valve machine, in the Netherlands in October 1939 and copied it to create the Model XA. The XA copied the BMW's horizontally opposed engine, shaft drive, and rear suspension (existing Harley-Davidsons had rigidly mounted rear wheels), modified for manufacturing with the inch measurements used in the US instead of the metric measurements used in Europe. A 1943 version also copied the BMW's telescopic front suspension. The Indian 841 used a unique 90-degree V-twin engine that was narrower than the BMW opposed twin layout, shaft drive, hydraulically damped girder front fork, and rear suspension. The 841 also had a foot gearshift and hand clutch, common in Europe by the late 1930s and used in all modern production motorcycles, which was easier to use than the hand gearshift and foot clutch used in contemporaneous Harley-Davidsons and Indians.[8]

The deciding factor in the Army's choice between existing and new motorcycle designs was the development of the Jeep. The Army had issued a request to the US automobile industry for a ¼-ton four-wheel-drive vehicle in July 1940. A competition immediately ensued between the small American Bantam Car Company, the midsized Willys-Overland, and the giant Ford Motor Company, which in July 1941 resulted in the Willys-Overland design becoming the standard vehicle, with elements incorporated from the American Bantam and Ford designs. Willys-Overland and Ford produced over 640,000 Jeeps from July 1941 through the end of the war, and the Jeep became the legendary all-purpose vehicle of the US armed forces. The versatility and numbers of the Jeep made motorcycles unnecessary for all but a few roles. Investment in new motorcycle designs that were unproven, were more expensive to produce, and would require months of preparation before full-scale production could begin became an extravagance under wartime resource limitations, so in July 1943, the Army dropped the XA and 841 projects after the production of just over 1,000 test samples of each model.[9]

Delco motor trike, showing its horizontally opposed two-cylinder engine and telescopic forks. *Courtesy of motorcycle-74.blogspot.com*

Indian 741 of the 701st Military Police Battalion at the Presidio in 1950. *Courtesy of the US Army Military Police Corps Regimental Museum*

The WLA, with "A" standing for "Army," became the uncontested standard Army motorcycle with the end of the XA and 841 programs. Production of the WLA had begun in January 1940, and under multiple Army contracts issued in 1940 and 1941, Harley-Davidson produced 421 WLAs in 1940 and 2,451 in 1941. In January 1942, immediately after the attack on Pearl Harbor, the Army awarded Harley-Davidson a contract for 31,393 WLAs, to be completed by December 31, 1943.[10] The 1942 model was the definitive WLA, produced from 1942 to 1945 with only minor changes and constituting the majority of the motorcycles in the Army's inventory. Harley-Davidson would produce 57,565 WLAs during the war, and a total of 88,000 military motorcycles of all types. Out of wartime WLA production, 23,403 went to the US armed forces, while 34,162—almost 60 percent—went to other Allied nations under Lend-Lease and other military assistance programs.

Indian produced military motorcycles primarily for export after losing the Army competition to Harley-Davidson. Indian offered its large Chief for military sales as the 340B, later renamed the 344, along with a 45-cubic-inch version of the 640 called the 640B, later renamed the 741. Indian achieved only limited US military sales, selling 2,943 340B/344s and 2,524 640B/741s to the US armed services, less than a quarter of their 23,403 WLAs. Indian produced a total of 42,044 military motorcycles of all types, half as many as Harley-Davidson.[11]

The WLA that emerged in 1942 from the evolution of the Forty-Five during the 1930s and the Army competition of 1939–1941 was large, heavy, and not well designed for off-road use, but it was simple, rugged, and durable. It was longer than most other military motorcycles and also heavier at 540 pounds empty, and it had limited ground clearance. A hand-shift transmission with only three speeds made extracting the engine's available power awkward. On the other hand, the WLA's unstressed and thoroughly debugged side-valve engine was reliable and simple to maintain and repair, with a low compression ratio (5.0:1) that made starting easy and allowed the engine to run on low-octane gasoline. The transmission, frame, and other cycle parts were similarly proven and durable. Another significant positive attribute of the WLA was the level of comfort made possible by its weight and spring-suspended seat, which allowed the rider to arrive less tired and more ready for action than riders of other machines. The WLA was somewhat bulky and lacking in performance on paper, but like its civilian ancestor, it was a dependable and effective machine in real-world use.

The characteristics of the WLA stood in sharp contrast to those of British military motorcycles. Like the WLA, British military motorcycles were civilian models with minor modifications to make them more suitable for military use. They were smaller and lighter than the WLA, with greater ground clearance. The typical British military motorcycle had a 500 cc or 350 cc single-cylinder engine, a four-speed foot shift transmission, and chain final drive; had a girder fork front suspension and no rear suspension; was about 7 feet in length with a wheelbase of less than 55 inches; and weighed less than 400 pounds.[12] The smaller dimensions, greater ground clearance, and lighter weight of the British machines gave them an advantage over the WLA in off-road mobility. The small engines and frames of these machines made them less capable of hauling a fully equipped soldier and gear, however, and their light weight and generally unsophisticated suspension systems made them rougher and more tiring to ride over long distances. Although faster and more maneuverable than the WLA, British military motorcycles were in important ways less suitable for the harsh conditions of a world war.

The German armed forces used a wide range of motorcycles, many of which had significant technical advantages over their US and British counterparts. The tactics and organization of the German army, the Wehrmacht, called for the use of large numbers of motorcycles for reconnaissance and for transporting mounted infantry, as well as for courier duty and general transportation. The Wehrmacht took into service numerous existing commercial models to fill out its force structure during its rapid rearmament in the 1930s, with its preferred models being from BMW and Zündapp. BMW and Zündapp each produced a range of motorcycles in the size classes considered large (750 cc) and medium (350–500 cc) in Germany, with horizontally opposed engines and shaft drive.

Misplaced priorities emerged when the Wehrmacht developed a motorcycle designed specifically for military use, with the adoption of complicated designs that were costly to produce. In 1937, the Wehrmacht contacted BMW and Zündapp with ambitious design goals for a motorcycle-and-sidecar combination capable of serving as an all-terrain scout and troop carrier vehicle, including the ability to carry a 500-kilogram (1,102 pound) payload, the equivalent of three fully equipped soldiers and their gear; a top speed of 95 kilometers per hour (59 mph), a cruising speed of 80 kph (50 mph), and a crawl speed of 4 kph (2.5 mph), the same speed as troops marching on foot; and minimum ground clearance of 150 mm (5.9 inches). Cost was no object in this request, and BMW and Zündapp each came up with a design that took full advantage of this generosity.

BMW R75. *Courtesy of Wikimedia*

The BMW R75 and Zündapp KS 750 each used an engine derived from an existing design but otherwise were entirely original, with a completely new frame, transmission, final drive system, and braking system. Each was an engineering tour de force with systems never before used on a motorcycle: four-speed transmission with high- and low-range gearing and reverse, giving eight forward speeds and two in reverse; powered sidecar wheel with a differential lock for low-traction situations; and three wheel brakes with hydraulic power assistance, when all other motorcycles and many automobiles still used simple cable- or rod-operated brakes. The power-assisted brakes were necessary to stop these massive machines, which weighed over 600 pounds without a sidecar and approximately 925 pounds with a sidecar.

The Wehrmacht acquired the R75 and KS 750 at great expense, although it faced a severe shortage of motor vehicles, and the majority of its units had to rely on horses. The Germans expended

Zündapp KS750. *Courtesy of Wikimedia*

valuable materials and skilled labor on these sophisticated machines, capable of carrying only three soldiers and little equipment, even though from 1940 onward they had an equivalent to the Jeep, the Volkswagen-based Kübelwagen ("bucket car"). The Wehrmacht simultaneously developed both the Kübelwagen and two types of specialized motorcycles and kept all three in full-scale production. BMW and Zündapp produced the R75 and KS 750 from 1941 to 1944, producing 18,000 of each model, until Allied strategic bombing damaged the BMW and Zündapp factories too badly for production to continue. Meanwhile, German industry produced only 50,450 Kübelwagens from 1940 to 1945, a small fraction of the over 640,000 Jeeps produced from 1941 to 1945.

The WLA with its lightly modified prewar civilian design lacked the innovative engineering and superior off-road performance of the Germans' specialized military motorcycles, but it did not need them. The WLA had more than adequate capability to perform the roles given to it by the US armed services. These roles were firmly established by 1943 and would remain consistent through the end of the war.

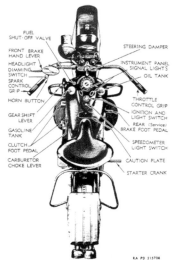

Overhead view of a 1942 WLA from the 1943 War Department technical manual for the WLA (TM 9-879). *Author's collection*

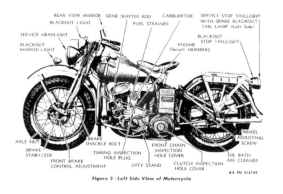

Side view of a 1942 WLA from the 1943 War Department technical manual for the WLA (TM 9-879). *Author's collection*

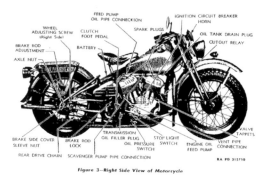

Side view of a 1942 WLA from the 1943 War Department technical manual for the WLA (TM 9-879). *Author's collection*

CHAPTER 2
Preparing for War

US military usage of the WLA in the Second World War followed a quarter century of experience and experimentation that went back to before the First World War. By the time that US ground forces engaged in major operations, they had ceased to use motorcycles as frontline combat vehicles, but the machines continued to serve in noncombat and support roles on all fronts.

The US Army had been one of the early military adopters of the motorcycle, acquiring its first motorcycles in 1913. These early machines saw action in the expedition pursuing Pancho Villa into Mexico in 1916. During the First World War, the US motorcycle industry supplied large numbers of machines to the US military, with over 20,000 Harley-Davidsons and Indians shipped overseas.[1]

The Army issued them to the newly created Motor Transport Corps, military police, signals units, and infantry and artillery units as general-purpose transportation.[2] An Army motorcyclist, Cpl. Roy Holtz, has been credited as the first American soldier to enter Germany during the pursuit of Germany's defeated army at the end of the First World War.

15th Military Police Company, 15th Cavalry Division, at Fort Bliss, Texas, in 1919. *Courtesy of the US Army Military Police Corps Regimental Museum*

Military police Harley-Davidson with sidecar at Fort Benning, Georgia. *Courtesy of the US Army Military Police Corps Regimental Museum*

61st Coast Artillery Regiment moving through Richmond, Virginia, on May 15, 1930. *Courtesy of the US Army Transportation Corps Museum*

Marine Corps motorcycle squad in Tientsin, China, during the 1920s. *Courtesy of the National Archives*

Marines on motorcycles with sidecars, armed with Thompson submachine guns, in Nicaragua in November 1928. *Courtesy of the National Archives*

Motorcyclist leads World War I–era M1917 tanks of the 3rd Marine Brigade in Tientsin during the late 1920s. *Courtesy of the National Archives*

WILDER MONUMENT OF CHICKAMAUGA BATTLEFIELD,
WITH MECHANIZED TROOPS IN FOREGROUND,
CHATTANOOGA, TENN.—71

Eggleston   Chesser   Cotton   Dyke   Dill

6th Cavalry Regiment troopers with motorcycles and M3 Scout Cars on the Civil War battlefield of
Chickamauga. Second from the right is Pvt. Beecher Dyke, profiled further on pages 80–83.
Courtesy of Jack Dyke

Between the world wars, the Army continued to use motorcycles in the same roles as during the First World War. The main users were military police and the Quartermaster Corps, for personnel escorting and directing supply convoys and other road traffic. Motorcycles were useful because of their ability to move around traffic, on narrow trails, and over terrain impassable to the primitive two-wheel-drive vehicles of the time. A military police company of five officers and 200 enlisted men, under the organization adopted in October 1918, had eighteen motorcycles as its motor transport, along with fifty horses, six draft mules, one wagon, and 105 bicycles.[3]

The Marine Corps also used motorcycles between the world wars in its overseas operations in China and Latin America. The basic Marine expeditionary unit in peacetime during the 1920s and 1930s was the reinforced infantry brigade, a combined arms formation with two infantry regiments, tanks, artillery, engineers, military police, and an attached Marine aviation squadron. Under the 1929 organization table, a brigade numbered 4,698 officers and enlisted men, with five tanks, twelve 75 mm howitzers, twenty-three aircraft, and 168 trucks. Each brigade would have thirty-four motorcycles with sidecars, performing a wide variety of roles in many of the brigade's units: ten in each infantry regiment, one with the engineer company, two with the military police company, one with the tank platoon, eighteen in the artillery battalion, and two with the aviation squadron.[4] A reorganization in 1939 increased the size of the reinforced infantry brigade to 7,116 officers and enlisted men, with eighteen tanks, twenty-four 75 mm howitzers, and 114 trucks. It took the motorcycles out of the infantry regiments but continued to use thirty in other units in the brigade, with one in the artillery regiment, five in the engineer battalion, and twenty-four in the transport company.[5]

As the Army prepared for the war on the horizon from the late 1930s to 1941, it briefly considered giving motorcycles a combat role in the mechanized cavalry. At the end of the 1930s, the Army still used horse cavalry as its force for reconnaissance, pursuit, and screening, having experimented with tanks, armored cars, and other motor vehicles since the 1920s without finally mechanizing the cavalry. After the German blitzkrieg through

Cavalry horses boarding their tractor-trailer transporters. *Courtesy of the National Archives*

Cavalry horses approach their tractor-trailer transporters, passing a group of three motorcycles.
Courtesy of the National Archives

Poland in September 1939, the Army decided to mechanize the cavalry to prepare it to support armored operations in Europe. Army cavalry units began in 1940 to experiment with the use of motorcycles, armored scout cars, and half-tracks as they worked to establish new doctrine, organization, and equipment for mechanized cavalry.

The cavalry arm converted a number of its regiments into part horse units and part mechanized units for these tests. Two of the Regular Army's fourteen horse cavalry regiments, the 4th and 6th Cavalry Regiments, became partially mechanized units immediately after the German invasion of Poland in 1939. Similarly, seven of the National Guard's seventeen horse cavalry regiments became partially mechanized in 1940–41: the 101st Cavalry in New York, the 102nd Cavalry in New Jersey, the 104th Cavalry in Pennsylvania, the 106th Cavalry in Illinois, the 107th Cavalry in Ohio, the 113th Cavalry in Iowa, and the 115th Cavalry in Wyoming.

The horse/mechanized cavalry regiment employed a mix of horse cavalry, armored scout cars, and motorcycles, to test the characteristics of each and determine the optimum combination for units performing the cavalry's missions. Each had a horse squadron with three cavalry troops (Troops A, B, and C), with the horses assisted by tractor-trailer transporters that carried them on long road marches to enable them to keep up with the motor vehicles. A mechanized squadron had two scout car troops (Troops D and E) and one motorcycle troop (Troop F). A headquarters troop and a service troop responsible for supply and equipment maintenance completed each regiment. (In cavalry terminology, a squadron is the equivalent of a battalion, and a troop is the equivalent of a company.)

These horse/mechanized cavalry regiments used considerable numbers both of horses and motor vehicles. Under the table of organization and equipment adopted in November 1940, each regiment of 1,591 officers and enlisted personnel had 68 armored scout cars, 177 motorcycles, 574 horses, 74 tractor-trailer horse transporters, 30 ½-ton trucks, and 45 2½-ton trucks.[6] The 177 motorcycles in each horse/mechanized regiment performed a variety of roles. Riflemen would ride motorcycles with sidecars in the motorcycle company of the mechanized squadron. (Motorcycles with sidecars were intended as substitutes for the motor trikes that were under development during the early 1940s, as described in chapter 1. The Army did not acquire either motor trikes or sidecars in substantial numbers, so the cavalry regiments used motorcycles without sidecars during the trials.) Scouts, messengers, mechanics, and officers and noncommissioned officers also rode motorcycles in the mechanized squadron, headquarters platoon, and service troop.

The Army tested the horse/mechanized cavalry regiments in maneuvers from 1940 to late 1941. The maneuvers tested the capabilities of the horse cavalry, armored scout cars, and riflemen on motorcycles, and their ability to operate together in varying terrain and combat situations. Motor vehicles, rapidly developing technologically both as heavy armored vehicles and lighter and faster motorcycles, competed against the familiar centuries-old horse cavalry on roads and off-road, in weather conditions including

Vehicle	Mechanized Squadron	Horse Squadron	Headquarters Squadron	Service Troop	Medical Detachment	TOTAL
Scout Car	48		17	3		68
Motorcycle, solo	84		16	14		114
Motorcycle, with sidecar	39		5	17	2	63
Horse		555			19	574
Truck, ½ ton, command	3		3	9		15
Truck, 2½ ton, cargo	12		6	27		45
Truck-tractor, with semitrailer				74		74
Truck, 4 ton, wrecker				1		1
Ambulance					2	2

Mechanized cavalry in M3 Scout Cars greeting cavalry horses, with a WLA and motorcycle riflemen behind them. *Courtesy of the National Archives*

Motorcycle riflemen on maneuvers, following an M3 Scout Car armed with three Browning M1917 water-cooled machine guns. *Courtesy of the National Archives*

Motorcycle riflemen dismounting and going into action on foot, supported by machine gunners in an M3 scout car. *Courtesy of the National Archives*

Motorcyclist on a WLA wearing the gold leather helmet, passing an M2 light tank. *Courtesy of the National Archives*

Motorcyclist training at Fort Knox in 1942 starting the horse cavalry slide maneuver, screaming as he hits the ground. *Courtesy of the National Archives*

Motorcyclist wearing a gas mask completing a jump on a WLA. The WLA is equipped with saddlebags and a rifle scabbard, here carrying a Thompson submachine gun. *Courtesy of the National Archives*

rain and snow, and in reconnoitering and then fighting after contact.

Motorcyclists used tactics similar to those of the horse cavalry, since they were similarly riding solo on individual vehicles operating in groups. They practiced similar movements in columns on roads and lines across country, and they trained when ambushed to use an old horse cavalry maneuver in which a rider would ride at full gallop, drop his horse to the ground, slide it to a stop on its side, and bring his weapon into action from its scabbard while using the horse as cover. Because of the hazards of executing these maneuvers, their riding gear included gold-colored leather crash helmets, later taken away and reissued to tank crews—the "gold football helmet" referenced in the 1970 movie *Patton*.

The maneuvers proved that both horses and motorcycles were unsuited for the future cavalry role. Horses and motor vehicles operated at different speeds, too differently to complement each other, and the tractor-trailer horse transporters that were necessary for the horses to keep up were unwieldy and difficult to maneuver. The motorcycles had significant limitations as well, for reasons obvious to anyone familiar with motorcycles. Motorcycles and their riders were highly vulnerable on the battlefield, and the machines of the time had been designed primarily for use on roads and performed poorly off-road. Moreover, they could not handle mud or snow. The 4th Cavalry concluded that "[t]he motorcycle is absolutely useless for reconnaissance over snow covered ground," finding that an inch of packed snow made their riders completely preoccupied with falling and incapable of reconnoitering, and that snow greater than 5 inches deep completely stopped them.[7] An officer of the 101st Cavalry remarked that the replacement of motorcycles with Jeeps "was a relief to many of those who had risked their lives riding them in the snow of New England and mud of the Carolinas."[8]

A 2nd Armored Division column of WLAs and a Jeep moving along a dirt road on maneuvers in North Carolina in 1942. *Courtesy of the National Archives*

Fully mechanized cavalry riding Jeeps and armored vehicles, not motorcycles, would be what the US Army used during the Second World War, and the Jeep further took the place of motorcycles throughout the Army and other US armed services. All fourteen Regular Army cavalry regiments became mechanized cavalry or armor units in 1940–43, and all seventeen National Guard cavalry regiments fully mechanized upon entering federal service. The Army began the war with motorcycles in the official Tables of Organization and Equipment (TO&Es) for its cavalry regiments, armored divisions, infantry divisions, and other combat and support units, but by 1943 the Army's TO&Es completely replaced motorcycles with Jeeps in almost all of its combat and support units. The Marine Corps would do the same by 1944.

The WLA and other motorcycles would go overseas with US soldiers and Marines during the war, but they would do so in support and unconventional roles rather than as main vehicles of combat units. Period photographs showing formations of motorcycles moving cross-country, machines leaping over obstacles, and riders armed with Thompson submachine guns would predominate after the war, but these uses of motorcycles in maneuvers were a dead end, with little relevance to the real war fought by US soldiers and Marines in 1941–45. US military WLAs would mostly plod around the rear echelons, carrying military police or messengers, with the ordinary M1 rifles and M1 carbines carried by infantrymen and support troops replacing the Thompson guns in the scabbards. These WLAs would perform vital but mostly unglamorous roles during the war in Europe and Asia.

M2 light tank of the 2nd Armored Division on maneuvers in North Carolina in 1942. *Courtesy of the National Archives*

African American motorcycle scout with a WLA on maneuvers at Fort Custer, Michigan, in August 1942. *Courtesy of the National Archives*

African American military policeman on a WLA. *Courtesy of the National Archives*

WLAs, Jeeps, and M3 Scout Cars
of the 101st Cavalry Regiment,
New York National Guard,
on maneuvers in May 1942.
*Courtesy of the New York
State Military Museum*

101st Cavalry Regiment troopers
on maneuvers in May 1942,
wearing leather helmets and
horse cavalry breeches.
*Courtesy of the New York
State Military Museum*

WLAs, Jeeps, and M3A1 Scout Cars of the 107th Cavalry Regiment, Ohio National Guard, at Fort Ord, California, in May 1942. *Courtesy of the National Archives*

PFC Harold Dearborn of the 100th Cavalry Reconnaissance Troop, 100th Infantry Division, goes airborne on his WLA during maneuvers at Fort Jackson, South Carolina, in 1943. *Courtesy of the National Archives*

The horse cavalry slide maneuver demonstrated by PFC Edward Mueller of the 100th Cavalry Reconnaissance Troop at Fort Jackson in 1943. He is sliding his motorcycle onto its left side, and preparing to dive behind it as cover and draw his weapon from its scabbard. *Courtesy of the National Archives*

The maneuver executed successfully by PFC Mueller. Note that the trooper to the left appears to be lying down in pain after executing the maneuver unsuccessfully. *Courtesy of the National Archives*

PFCs Nelligan, Mueller, Priest, Paskowitz, Kowalski, and Dearborn of the 100th Cavalry Reconnaissance Troop, 100th Infantry Division, on their WLAs at Fort Jackson, South Carolina, in 1943. *Courtesy of the National Archives*

CHAPTER 3

The WLA in the US Army

The decision not to use motorcycles as mechanized cavalry vehicles and the adoption of the Jeep resulted in the WLA receiving limited roles that officially went away by the end of the war in most units of the US Army. The mechanized cavalry retained only a fraction of the number of motorcycles used in 1940 in the TO&E for mechanized cavalry regiments that the Army adopted in 1942, and all motorcycles disappeared in a further reorganization in 1943. Armored divisions likewise included small numbers of motorcycles in their 1942 TO&E and eliminated them in 1943. Infantry divisions similarly eliminated all motorcycles by 1943, as did independent tank battalions. Tank destroyer battalions with self-propelled guns kept them until 1944, while battalions with towed guns kept them until the end of the war. The most substantial use of motorcycles was in military police units, which kept them in service throughout the war.

Despite the disappearance of motorcycles from the official TO&Es of most units from 1943 onward, WLAs remained in service with many of those units until the end of the war. Many units retained them after the Army eliminated them from their standard unit organization, preferring to keep familiar vehicles already in their inventory rather than turn them in. As a result, the WLA continued to appear in frontline service in 1944–45 with combat units that were no longer supposed to use them.

Units that continued to use the WLA in 1944–45 in some instances used them in numbers exceeding any previously authorized levels. For example, military police units commonly used many times more WLAs than they had been originally issued, even after they were supposed to have replaced them with Jeeps. An oversupply of motorcycles after most units ceased to use them and returned them to depots made it possible.

Lt. Col. William Darby, founder of the modern Army Rangers, on a WLA outside the city hall of Arzew, Algeria, in November 1942, during the 1st Ranger Battalion's first action during Operation Torch. Darby's M1903 Springfield rifle is visible in the scabbard. *Courtesy of the National Archives*

Pvt. Harold Peters of the 6th Cavalry Group riding a WLA on a road turned into mud near Nancy, France, on October 2, 1944. He wears a tank crewman's helmet and has an M1 Carbine slung over his shoulder, with no front fender scabbard. *Courtesy of the National Archives*

Excess WLAs were available even though the Army canceled a substantial percentage of its order for WLAs in 1944 and began to sell its inventory of WLAs as surplus before the end of the war. In February 1944, the Army reduced deliveries under its contract with Harley-Davidson by 12,436—approximately a third of its original wartime order for WLAs. The Army also declared 4,600 of its motorcycles in the continental United States to be surplus and for sale to the public in the spring of 1944, then announced the sale of another 3,500 in August 1944.[1] More than sufficient numbers of motorcycles were already overseas in Europe and the Pacific to meet the needs of US forces.

Mechanized Cavalry Regiments/Groups

The cavalry reduced the roles and numbers of motorcycles in the TO&E for mechanized cavalry regiments dated April 1, 1942, then dropped them entirely in the definitive wartime TO&E dated September 15, 1943. The mechanized cavalry used the 1942 organization in the North Africa campaign from November 1942 to May 1943, then fought the campaign in northern Europe from D-day to the end of the war with the 1943 TO&E.

The new mechanized cavalry regiment of 1942 was fully mechanized and considerably more powerful than its predecessor, with light tanks, self-propelled artillery on half-tracks, and Jeeps armed with machine guns. It was a flexible organization with two squadron headquarters and a mix of units—four reconnaissance troops with armored cars and Jeeps, and two support troops with light tanks and self-propelled artillery—that could be combined into task forces under each squadron headquarters. Each regiment of 1,642 officers and enlisted personnel now had fifty-five motorcycles, less than a third of the 177 used previously, all designated for support instead of combat roles. There were sixteen in the headquarters troop, three in the service troop, two in each squadron headquarters, and eight in each reconnaissance troop.

The Army formed fifteen mechanized cavalry regiments, eight as Regular Army units (2nd, 3rd, 4th, 6th, 11th, 14th, 15th, 16th) and seven as National Guard units (101st, 102nd, 104th, 106th, 107th, 113th, 115th). They included all the units that had been horse/mechanized units in 1940–41: the 4th Cavalry, the 6th Cavalry, and the seven National Guard cavalry regiments.

The 1943 reorganization redesignated the mechanized cavalry regiments as identically numbered mechanized cavalry groups and made the two squadrons under them more self-supporting, with support elements transferred from the regiment to the squadron level. Each squadron had a headquarters and service troop, three reconnaissance troops with M8 armored cars and Jeeps, a company of M5 light tanks, and a troop of M8 assault guns, as well as attached medical personnel. Jeeps replaced motorcycles in all roles previously filled by them. Motorcycles lacked the cross-country mobility of the 4 × 4 Jeeps, 6 × 6 M8 armored cars, and tracked M5 light tanks and M8 assault guns, which was essential to the reconnaissance mission.

Armored Divisions

The US Army's armored divisions used three TO&Es during World War II, two of which saw action during the war. An early TO&E

Pvt. Robert J. Vance, a dispatch rider with the 2nd Armored Division, during the breakout from Normandy at St. Lô on July 22, 1944. Vance had been caught in an artillery barrage while delivering messages and had to take cover for forty-five minutes before getting through. *Courtesy of the National Archives*

Motorcycle messengers Pvt. Lambert Keeler, Pvt. Robert Wise, Pvt. Orval Foster, and Pvt. Charles Haugland of the 2nd Armored Division work on their WLAs near Carentan in Normandy in July 1944. *Courtesy of the National Archives*

dated November 15, 1940, provided the initial basis for the organization of the first US armored divisions. A new TO&E dated March 1, 1942, saw service in the North Africa campaign, then until the end of the war with two "heavy" armored divisions. All other armored divisions used the smaller "light" armored division TO&E adopted on September 15, 1943.

The 1940 armored division was an armor-heavy formation that was never fully implemented in any division. It had eight tank battalions and two armored infantry battalions and a total of 12,697 officers and men, with 381 tanks and 2,851 other vehicles. Predating the introduction of the Jeep, it would have used 520 motorcycles and 290 motor tricycles, a quarter of the division's total vehicles.

The 1942 "heavy" armored division was a more balanced formation that used the more up-to-date equipment that had become available by 1942. With six tank battalions and three infantry battalions, totaling 14,620 officers and men, it was a flexible organization with three "combat commands," each of which could control any combination of the division's units necessary for a specific mission. Each division now had 390 tanks and 2,928 other vehicles, with 524 Jeeps and only 204 motorcycles.

The 1943 "light" armored division was a smaller formation that was even less tank heavy than the 1942 armored division. With three tank battalions and three armored infantry battalions, it had 263 tanks and 10,937 officers and men. It carried further the modernization of equipment in the 1942 armored division, finally eliminating all motorcycles and instead using 462 Jeeps.[2]

The Army formed sixteen armored divisions during the Second World War, numbered 1st through 14th, 16th, and 20th. The 1st through 5th Armored Divisions formed in 1940–41 under the 1940 TO&E, then transitioned to the 1942 "heavy" armored division TO&E. All other armored divisions formed in 1942–43 under the 1942 TO&E. The 1st and 2nd Armored Divisions fought in the North Africa campaign organized under the 1942 TO&E. When the transition to the 1943 armored division TO&E occurred, fourteen armored divisions adopted it, while the 2nd and 3rd Armored Divisions retained the 1942 TO&E.

Although motorcycles disappeared from the official equipment inventory of armored divisions transitioning to the 1943 TO&E, and the 2nd and 3rd Armored Divisions probably eliminated many or most of them as Jeeps became available, many remained in service with armored divisions of both types until the end of the war.

Cpl. Gordon Powell of the 82nd Armored Reconnaissance Battalion, 2nd Armored Division, on a WLA
(*left*) and British Army XXX Corps dispatch rider Baltins Dogoughs on a Norton 16H with a missing front
fender (*right*) meeting at Pacy-Sur-Eure, on August 27, 1944. *Courtesy of the National Archives*

T/5 Charles Parker, a scout in the reconnaissance group of the 1st Infantry Division, in Sicily in July 1943. *Courtesy of the National Archives*

Infantry Divisions

The infantry division was the main unit of the US Army during the Second World War, as it was in all other armies. The US Army formed sixty-six infantry divisions, the majority of the eighty-nine divisions that it formed during the war. The infantry division went through several changes in organization from 1939 to 1941 as the Army prepared for war, then three more from 1942 to 1945. Motorcycles were officially eliminated from the infantry division TO&E by 1943.

Prewar US Army infantry divisions were "square" divisions that differed significantly from the "triangular" division used during the war. With two infantry brigades of two infantry regiments each, they were large but unwieldy, and the smaller but more maneuverable triangular division of three regiments replaced it by 1942. The prewar square divisions used large numbers of motorcycles, with the September 1939 TO&E having 278 (4 solo, 274 with sidecars) in each division of 18,302 officers and enlisted men, and the November 1940 TO&E having 308 (21 solo, 287 with sidecars) in a division totaling 22,272.[3] The triangular infantry division adopted in October 1939 was considerably smaller, totaling

only 8,960 officers and enlisted men. Each had 133 motorcycles with sidecars.[4] There were five infantry divisions in the Regular Army in 1939 and ten by 1940, with additional divisions activated froWhen the Army adopted its definitive wartime structure of triangular infantry divisions in August 1942, the organization and equipment of the division changed significantly as battlefield requirements became clearer and equipment became available. Each division now had 15,514 officers and enlisted men.[5] With the Jeep now entering the Army's inventory in large numbers, each division now had 496 Jeeps, taking most of the roles formerly filled by motorcycles. There were now only twenty-nine solo motorcycles in each division, with nine in the division reconnaissance group, eighteen in the engineer battalion, and two in the military police platoon.[6]

A revised TO&E in July 1943 eliminated all the remaining motorcycles from the infantry divisions.[7] As in the armored divisions, motorcycles remained in use in many infantry divisions into 1945, however, with units retaining machines issued earlier instead of turning in all of them with each reorganization.

The rider of a WLA attempts to negotiate a demolished mountain road in Sicily, August 1943. *Courtesy of the National Archives*

T/5 Raymond Powell, a messenger in the 315th Engineer Battalion, 90th Infantry Division, checks his bearings in the Saar region of Germany in November 1944. He is wearing a captured German rubberized motorcyclist suit and has an M1 Garand rifle in his WLA's weapon scabbard. *Courtes of the National Archives*

Cavalry Divisions and Regiments

The 1st Cavalry Division and other nonmechanized cavalry units had unique organizations as horse cavalry, but they fought in the Pacific theater as dismounted infantry. The 1st Cavalry Division, formed in 1921, had three distinct cavalry division TO&Es issued in November 1940, August 1942, and September 1944 but fought overseas as a "Special" cavalry division with a nonstandard infantry organization. The 2nd Cavalry Division, formed in April 1941 as a unique racially integrated unit in the then-segregated Army, both with segregated African American and regular cavalry regiments, was deactivated in July 1942, again formed in February 1943, but then disbanded again in North Africa in early 1944. Two separate cavalry regiments, the 112th and 124th Cavalry Regiments of the Texas National Guard, served to the end of the war, similarly to the 1st Cavalry Division.

The cavalry division TO&E dated November 1, 1940, was for an organization with 11,676 men, 7,699 horses, and 295 mules, with motor vehicles in scout and support roles. It was a "square" division, with two cavalry brigades, each with two cavalry regiments of two cavalry battalions. It included 239 motorcycles and 135 motor tricycles, along with 13 light tanks, 148 scout cars, 3 half-tracks, 702 trucks, and 11 cars.[8]

The revised TO&E dated August 1, 1942, followed the lead of the armored and infantry divisions in substituting Jeeps and other new vehicles for motorcycles. Now with 12,112 soldiers, 6,999 horses, and 299 mules, a cavalry division would have 454 Jeeps and only forty-one motorcycles. There were 17 light tanks, 64 armored cars, 26 scout cars, 10 half-tracks, and 696 trucks. The forty-one motorcycles consisted of twenty-six in the reconnaissance squadron, thirteen in the engineer squadron, and two in the military police platoon.[9]

A final cavalry division TO&E dated September 30, 1944, never implemented while the 1st Cavalry Division was deployed overseas as dismounted infantry, eliminated all motorcycles except for the two in the military police platoon. Theoretically, it would have had 11,216 soldiers, 7,703 horses, 294 mules, 17 light tanks, 5 M8 75 mm gun motor carriages, 93 armored cars, 10 scout cars, 27 half-tracks, 438 Jeeps, and 549 trucks.[10]

The 1st Cavalry Division and the 112th and 124th Cavalry Regiments fought overseas as Cavalry (Special) infantry units. The 1st Cavalry Division fought in the Admiralty Islands north of Papua New Guinea from February through May 1944, then in the Philippine campaign from October 1944 to July 1945. The only motorcycles in the TO&E from 1942 through 1945 were two in the military police platoon. They went away in a final reorganization at the end of the Philippine campaign in July 1945.[11]

Independent Tank and Tank Destroyer Battalions

The US Army formed numerous independent tank and tank destroyer battalions to augment and support its infantry and armored divisions as needed, and these battalions used numerous motorcycles in 1940–42.

Tank battalions used motorcycles as courier and support vehicles. Under TO&Es adopted in November 1940, each light-tank battalion of forty-two tanks had sixteen motorcycles, four in the battalion headquarters and twelve in the tank companies, and each medium-tank battalion of fifty-three tanks had thirteen, four in the battalion headquarters and nine in the tank companies.[12] In the light- and medium-tank battalion TO&Es adopted in March 1942, which increased tank strength to fifty-four in each battalion, each battalion headquarters continued to have four motorcycles, although the tank companies no longer had them.[13]

Tank destroyer battalions used motorcycles more extensively as scout vehicles as well as in courier and support roles. Under the TO&E adopted in December 1941, a light-tank-destroyer battalion with thirty-six towed 37 mm antitank guns had twenty-six motorcycles: ten in the battalion headquarters, four in each of the three tank destroyer companies, and four in the pioneer company.[14] Heavy-tank-destroyer battalions, each with twenty-four 3-inch and twelve 37 mm self-propelled antitank guns, had thirty-seven motorcycles, thirteen in the headquarters company, five in each of the three tank destroyer companies, and nine in the reconnaissance company.[15] A revised tank destroyer battalion TO&E adopted in June 1942 reduced the motorcycles to twenty-three, with eight in the headquarters company, two in each tank destroyer company, and nine in the reconnaissance company.[16]

Motorcycles went away from all the tank and tank destroyer battalions in 1943–44, except for towed tank destroyer battalions. Tank battalions ceased to use them under revised TO&Es adopted in late 1943.[17] Tank destroyer battalions with self-propelled tank destroyers continued to have fifteen each—four in the headquarters company, one in each tank destroyer company, and eight in reconnaissance company—under the TO&E adopted in January 1943, but eliminated them in March 1944.[18] Tank destroyer battalions with towed antitank guns continued to use them until the end of the war under the TO&E dated May 7, 1943. Each of these battalions, with thirty-six towed antitank guns, included eleven motorcycles as reconnaissance and courier vehicles. Two were in each of the battalion's two reconnaissance platoons, four were in the signals platoon, and each of the battalion's three companies of twelve antitank guns had one.[19]

M10 tank destroyer passing a WLA of the 28th Infantry Division in Percy, France, in Normandy between St. Lô and Avranches, during Operation Cobra on August 1, 1944. *Courtesy of the National Archives*

281st Military Police Company motorcycles, with the Rome Area Allied Command, lined up in front of the Colosseum in 1944. In this photograph, twenty-one motorcycles are visible. *Courtesy of the US Army Military Police Corps Regimental Museum*

The Army had sixty-five independent tank battalions and seventy-eight tank destroyer battalions at their peak in 1944.[20] There were thirty-seven independent tank battalions, thirty-two self-propelled tank destroyer battalions, and twenty-three towed tank destroyer battalions deployed to the European theater of operations.[21]

Military Police

Military police were significant users of motorcycles even after their withdrawal from combat units. With the missions of traffic control, the collection and processing of prisoners of war, maintaining security behind the front line, and addressing disciplinary problems,

military police needed the ability of motorcycles to move easily through traffic-choked roads. As a result, motorcycles remained in military police units at each level: in each division, a military police platoon; in each corps, a military police company; and in each field army, a military police battalion.

Division military police platoons used motorcycles extensively even when they were officially eliminated or in limited use. Armored division and infantry division TO&Es by 1943 dropped motorcycles from military police platoons, and airborne divisions had only two allocated to theirs. They were present in larger numbers than ever officially authorized in the military police

281st Military Police Company military policemen and motorcycles in front of the Colosseum in 1944.
Courtesy of the US Army Military Police Corps Regimental Museum

281st Military Police Company military policemen and motorcycles in Venice on the Piazza San Marco. *Courtesy of the US Army Military Police Corps Regimental Museum*

platoons of many divisions throughout the campaign in Europe in 1944–45, however, as many division commanders assigned extra personnel and equipment to their military police platoon after recognizing that the scale and difficulty of the military police mission were greater than anticipated by Army planners. For example, the 1st Infantry Division maintained a military police platoon of approximately 100 officers and enlisted men with up to fifteen motorcycles from D-day to the end of the war in Europe in May 1945.[22]

Military police companies and battalions in 1942 included motorcycles, which officially went away in 1943. A military police company had six motorcycles, two in the company headquarters and two in each of two traffic platoons, under the TO&E adopted in April 1942.[23] A military police battalion had twenty motorcycles, six in each military police company and an additional two in the battalion headquarters.[24] Jeeps replaced all these motorcycles in new TO&Es dated August 1943.[25] Nevertheless, motorcycles remained in service with these units until the end of the war, often in numbers far exceeding those authorized under the official 1942 TO&Es.

Military police companies specialized for aviation or post, camp, and station duty policed and provided security at airfields, bases, and other installations. Varying in size and composition, they included motorcycles in their authorized basic equipment. Under the TO&E adopted in May 1942, each company would have six motorcycles in its motorized section, along with two Jeeps and a 2½-ton truck.[26] Under a revised TO&E adopted in January 1945, the motorized section could have six to seventeen motorcycles.[27]

Military police escort guard companies did not officially include any motorcycles, but escorts for VIPs routinely included military police motorcyclists.[28]

Gen. Dwight D. Eisenhower with his staff car and two military police motorcycle escorts on WLAs. *Courtesy of the US Army Military Police Corps Regimental Museum*

Military police escorting an armored car carrying Generals George C. Marshall, Walter Bedell Smith, and J. Lawton Collins near the Siegfried Line at Kornelmünster, Germany, in the vicinity of Aachen, in October 1944. *Courtesy of the National Archives*

Pvt. James W. Carroll, 628th Tank Destroyer Battalion

Pvt. James Carroll of the 628th Tank Destroyer Battalion achieved a historic feat as the first American soldier to cross the border between France and Belgium and liberate the town of Peruwelz on September 3, 1944, riding a WLA.

Carroll served in the 628th Tank Destroyer Battalion, a self-propelled tank destroyer unit that landed at Utah Beach on July 30, 1944, as part of Gen. George S. Patton's 3rd Army. The battalion participated in the breakout from Normandy in Operation Cobra and in the liberation of Paris; drove across France, Belgium, and Luxembourg to the German border; participated in the Battle of the Huertgen Forest and the Battle of the Bulge; crossed the Rhine River; and reached the Elbe River on April 11, 1945. Carroll served as a motorcycle scout in a unit not officially issued any motorcycles, riding ahead of the battalion during advances.

A brief moment in Peruwelz on September 3, 1944, made Carroll a symbol of the liberation of the town and all of Belgium. With the battalion waiting in a forest at the Franco-Belgian border, Carroll received an order to cross the border and enter the town to scout for any German forces. Carroll entered the town in the morning, alone on his WLA, and found himself suddenly cut off when a column of German vehicles retreated down the main street. Seeing a German motorcyclist at the tail of the convoy stop and start shooting indiscriminately at house windows, Carroll became enraged and shot and killed the German for shooting at civilians. Riding back to his unit to report, he found a Belgian resistance group and returned to Peruwelz at about noon, with one of them riding on the back of his WLA. In the town, Carroll found a celebration in progress, and Belgian civilians draped his motorcycle in flowers and gave him a bottle of cognac. The battalion never entered the town, and Carroll almost immediately departed, his ride into Peruwelz left unrecorded in the unit's official history.[29]

For the people of Peruwelz, though, Carroll's arrival became an epic moment, the day of their liberation from four years of occupation by Nazi Germany. The legend grew after false news arrived that Carroll had been killed in action shortly after his ride through the town. Townspeople set up a photograph of him as a shrine in the town church, and each year they celebrated a Mass in his memory. Carroll became a legendary hero of the liberation as time passed.[30]

Carroll survived the war and served in the Army until 1965, retiring as a sergeant first class. Reentering civilian life, he worked for sixteen years as a librarian for the University of Minnesota and for a time served as the part-time mayor of the town where he lived. He returned to his native Alabama for his second retirement, settling in the town of Brewton, near his birthplace in Castleberry.

Carroll remained unaware of the reverence for him in Peruwelz for half a century, until citizens of the town tracked him down during the mid-1990s. In 1995, the town decided to find his grave and decorate it to commemorate the fiftieth anniversary of the end of the war in Europe. Failing to find any record of his burial, they turned to a US expert in locating servicemen, who found Carroll in Alabama in March 1996. By then seventy-five years of age, Carroll returned to the town for the first time in fifty-two years in May 1996, as the guest of honor at the town's celebration of Victory in Europe Day. He then returned each year to Belgium for its annual Victory in Europe Day celebration, spending three weeks each May attending an annual reenactment of his entry into Peruwelz, a banquet with the royal family of Belgium, and numerous other ceremonies as a living symbol of liberation from Nazi occupation.

The liberation of a Belgian town by an American soldier riding a WLA that beat long odds to be there was the work of a man who also beat long odds to be there, because James Carroll's early life and military service had him headed for trouble rather than a great wartime achievement. Born in 1921 to a prostitute in Castleberry, Alabama, he was adopted at the age of six by a Mr. and Mrs. Russell Carroll in Tampa, Florida. After the couple divorced, at age sixteen he joined a carnival that toured the South, and he was sent to a military school in Washington, DC, after stealing a car. After the attack on Pearl Harbor, Carroll found himself drafted into the Army, where he was, in his own words, "a good soldier" but "a little wild too." He went absent without leave for twenty-eight days to visit a girl in Texas. Carroll's commanding officer must have seen potential in him, because instead of a court-martial, he gave him the opportunity to volunteer for any duty that he wanted if he would promise to behave in the future. Carroll volunteered to ride motorcycles even though he had no experience riding them, and fate then cast him in the wartime role of a motorcycle scout in the 628th Tank Destroyer Battalion headed into Belgium.[31]

James Carroll died on June 28, 2005, at the age of eighty-three. He is buried at Fort Crawford Cemetery in Brewton, Alabama.

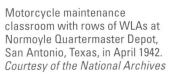

Motorcycle maintenance classroom with rows of WLAs at Normoyle Quartermaster Depot, San Antonio, Texas, in April 1942. *Courtesy of the National Archives*

1st Motorcycle Platoon, 760th Military Police Battalion, in the Panama Canal Zone in April 1942. *Courtesy of the US Army Military Police Corps Regimental Museum*

Military policemen Cpl. Albert Salem and SSgt. Charles Hicks escorting trucks across southern England in August 1943. *Courtesy of the National Archives*

MPs of the 196th Military Police Company in Leicester, England, in March 1944 demonstrating how to operate a motorcycle to Billy Smith, a seven-year-old whom they had befriended and given an artificial leg and sergeant's uniform after he lost a leg. *Courtesy of the National Archives*

Military police escort of Fifth Army commanding general Lt. Gen. Mark Clark, well equipped with white helmets, leather kidney belts, and Thompson submachine guns, in Mostaganem, Algeria, in August 1943. *Courtesy of the US Army Military Police Corps Regimental Museum*

Actress Martha Raye, entertaining US troops in North Africa, with military police motorcyclists in Casablanca in January 1943. *Courtesy of the US Army Military Police Corps Regimental Museum*

281st Military Police Company motorcyclists escorting a VIP in Italy. *Courtesy of the US Army Military Police Corps Regimental Museum*

US Army military police with WLAs, Italian Bersaglieri, and British army motorcyclists serving as the honor guard for Crown Prince Umberto of Italy during his visit to American Military Government headquarters in Bologna on April 25, 1945. *Courtesy of the National Archives*

Working on a military police WLA in Italy. *Courtesy of the US Army Military Police Corps Regimental Museum*

Kidding around on a military police WLA in Italy. *Courtesy of the US Army Military Police Corps Regimental Museum*

PFC Henry Murtaugh of the 202nd Military Police Company checking the papers of the driver of a captured Italian SPA TL 37 artillery tractor in May 1945. *Courtesy of the National Archives*

CHAPTER 4
Airborne Division Motorcycles

Airborne troops at Fort Benning, Georgia, boarding a mockup of a transport plane with their bicycles in April 1942. *Courtesy of the National Archives*

The US Army's airborne divisions were the exception to the phasing out of motorcycles from the Army's combat units during the war. The airborne divisions had unique requirements for light two-wheeled vehicles, because Jeeps and trucks were too large and heavy to drop by parachute, and gliders could not deliver them in sufficient numbers to meet the needs of airborne units in ground combat. When the airborne divisions formed in 1942–43—the 82nd and 101st Airborne Divisions in 1942, and the 11th, 13th, and 17th Airborne Divisions in 1943—they included numerous two-wheeled vehicles in their TO&Es to give greater mobility to units that critically needed it. The airborne divisions actually increased their use of motorcycles during the war, adding more WLAs and introducing new classes of light motorcycles as the years passed.

Bicycles were the initial solution to the problem of finding a vehicle that could be delivered by airdrop. The airborne division TO&E dated October 15, 1942, included eighty-one bicycles in each airborne division: twenty-nine in each of the two glider infantry regiments, ten in the engineer battalion, nine in the

signals company, and four in the medical company. Motorcycles also were present in small numbers, with the military police platoon having two. The units issued bicycles and the military police platoon landed by glider, so they could bring their vehicles and bulky equipment that would be difficult to deliver by parachute. The bicycles and motorcycles were part of a small pool of vehicles allocated to each 8,500-man airborne division, which included 299 Jeeps, twenty ¾-ton trucks, and eighty-two 2½-ton trucks.[1]

Motor scooters and motorized bicycles were the next solution in 1944. As of February 24, 1944, a change to the TO&E deleted the pedal-powered bicycles and substituted motor scooters, with each division to receive 205 scooters that would be used by almost all units in the division. The motor scooters were the Cushman Model 53, a lightweight (255-pound) machine with a prewar single-cylinder, 4.6-horsepower scooter engine in a stamped-steel frame. Designed to be dropped by parachute, the Model 53 could reach 40 miles per hour and tow a small cargo trailer, making it well suited to move quickly and transport essential gear in support of airborne units. A further addition was a small motorcycle called the Servicycle,

officially designated a motorized bicycle, which entered service in April 1943. The Servicycle was a motorcycle made by the Simplex Manufacturing Corporation since 1935, weighing only 135 pounds and powered by a 4-horsepower, 130 cc, two-stroke engine. The February 24, 1944, TO&E assigned nine Servicycles to the signal company of each airborne division. Two WLAs continued to be included in each divisional military police platoon.

The airborne divisions that dropped into Normandy on D-day also used motorcycles and other vehicles captured from the German forces, to make up for their limited motorized transport. The Kettenkrad tracked motorcycle in particular appears in numerous photographs of troops of the 82nd Airborne and 101st Airborne Divisions in Normandy. The Kettenkraftrad ("Tracked Motorcycle"), called Kettenkrad for short, was a utility vehicle that originally had been designed as a small artillery tractor for German airborne troops, deliverable by transport aircraft. The Kettenkrad may have appeared in photographs out of proportion to its actual numbers because of the novelty of the vehicle, which had no US equivalent and as a result may have frequently caught the attention of photographers.

Experience in airborne operations on D-day and later in the campaign in Europe led to successive increases in the numbers of motorcycles and other motor vehicles. A new airborne division TO&E adopted on August 1, 1944, just after the campaign in Normandy, increased the number of scooters to 236 while dropping the Servicycles. An airborne division TO&E dated December 16, 1944, after Operation Market-Garden, further increased the number of all types of vehicles in each airborne division and introduced a new extra-light motorcycle. The number of motorcycles increased to fourteen, and 246 extra-light motorcycles were to substitute for the scooters used earlier.[2] The number of Jeeps and trucks more than doubled in this reorganization. A final airborne division TO&E, adopted in the spring of 1945, used motorcycles as designated scout vehicles. The division reconnaissance platoon included twelve motorcycles, with each platoon having two scout sections, each with six motorcycles and seven Jeeps.[3]

These official reorganizations did not reflect actual usage in the field, which kept equipment in service after their supposed replacement and at times departed from the official TO&E. For example, the Servicycles continued in use at least through Operation Market-Garden in September 1944, as documented in photographs. The extra-light motorcycle, designated M1 and designed by Indian under the name Model 148, reached prototype stage by December 1944, but the War Department then canceled further development and did

101st Airborne Division troops with WLAs disembark from a Horsa glider after a training landing in the UK on May 12, 1944, less than a month before D-day. *Courtesy of the National Archives*

not acquire any.[4] Cushman Model 53 scooters and other vehicles continued to do the jobs intended for the M1 extra-light motorcycles.

The military police platoons of airborne divisions, like those of other types of divisions, became significantly larger than their official organizations in men and equipment, including motorcycles.

An airborne division military police platoon had an authorized strength of thirty-eight officers and enlisted personnel and two scooters or motorcycles, but the 82nd Airborne Division expanded its military police platoon to approximately eighty officers and enlisted personnel with at least nine motorcycles.[5]

Kettenkrad captured in Normandy, ridden by Pvt. Steve Barney of the 506th Parachute Infantry Regiment, 101st Airborne Division, in Carentan on June 17, 1944.
Courtesy of the National Archives

US paratroopers in Normandy ride a Kettenkrad through Sainte-Mère-Église on June 12, 1944.
Courtesy of the National Archives

Cushman scooter of the 82nd
Airborne Division under repair in
Holland in November 1944.
Courtesy of the National Archives

82nd Airborne Division MP Platoon
motorcycle squad with nine WLAs
on May 2, 1945. *Courtesy of the US
Army Military Police Corps
Regimental Museum*

CHAPTER 5
The WLA in the Pacific Theater

WLAs served in the Pacific theater as well as the European theater, in very different conditions than in Europe. The Pacific theater covered vast expanses of the Pacific Ocean and the Asian mainland, with long supply lines stretching across the Pacific, ground forces consisting both of Army and Marine Corps units fighting in the island-hopping campaign toward Japan, and US air forces supporting China's resistance against Japan from airbases scattered widely around China. WLAs performed valuable noncombat roles supporting these missions, from islands in the Pacific to the mountains of China-Burma-India.

The Army brought the same organizations to the Pacific theater that it brought to the European theater, and motorcycles served similar roles in the Army units sent to the Pacific. The ground war on Pacific islands and in Asia was fought mainly by infantry on foot, supported by small numbers of tanks (unlike the war in Europe, with armored divisions with hundreds of tanks and other vehicles), so there was little use for mechanized cavalry and other fast-moving motorized units. Instead, the vast distances and scattered bases in Asia and the Pacific required units in which motorcycles performed crucial roles. Military police of all types—divisional MP platoons, corps MP companies, army MP battalions, and aviation and post military police companies to guard airbases and other base areas; engineer battalions to build the Burma Road, Ledo Road, and other crucial supply lines; and other logistical support units—used numerous WLAs to perform their missions.

The Marine Corps, like the Army, planned to use motorcycles extensively in its combat units up to 1940 but curtailed their usage as Jeeps became available. As in Army units, motorcycles continued to be used in the military police and other units that considered them useful. Under the table of organization for the Marine Division, dated April 15, 1943, a division of 18,144 officers and enlisted men, reinforced by 1,821 Navy personnel, had only twelve motorcycles: one solo machine with the engineer regiment, two motorcycles with sidecars with the division headquarters battalion, one motorcycle with sidecar with the tank battalion, one motorcycle with sidecar with the military police platoon, five motorcycles with sidecars with the motor transport battalion, and two motorcycles with sidecars with the amphibious tractor battalion.[1] Motorcycles completely disappeared from the Marine Division table of organization dated May 5, 1944.[2] Nevertheless, WLAs continued to be used by military police and other units of the Marine Corps to the end of the war and beyond.

Motorcycles used in the Pacific theater included captured Harley-Davidson clones produced in Japan. Harley-Davidson had exported motorcycles to Japan for military use starting in 1917, then began assembling its Japanese-market machines locally during the Great Depression and licensed production to a Japanese company in 1933.[3] Production of the side-valve Harley-Davidson Model VL in Japan by Sankyo Seiyaku began in 1935, under the name Rikuo, meaning "Road King."[4] Wartime photographs show Marines repairing captured Imperial Japanese military Rikuos and putting them into service.

In an amphibious landing exercise in August 1941, Marine riflemen and machine gunners with a motorcycle and sidecar follow tanks inland. *Courtesy of the National Archives*

738th Military Police Company cycle patrol, Base Section 3, Brisbane, Australia, on April 12, 1943. *Courtesy of the National Archives*

Motorcycles and messengers of Base Section 3 Message Center, Somerville House, Brisbane, Australia, on November 9, 1943. *Courtesy of the National Archives*

Military police escorting a truck convoy preparing for movement, May 1945. *Courtesy of the National Archives*

Military police port patrol near cargo ships loaded with armored cars and trucks, May 1945. *Courtesy of the National Archives*

1st Lt. Chester Lamb, head of the Engineer Utilities Shop serving US Army installations in New Delhi, preparing for an inspection trip around the city on February 26, 1945. *Courtesy of the National Archives*

Capt. J. V. Bongiorno, Sgt. Harry Leffel, and Cpl. H. D. Stubbs of the 1211th Military Policy Company (Aviation) guarding the C-54 transport plane of Vice President Henry Wallace at the US airbase at Chungking, the wartime capital of Nationalist China, in June 1944. *Courtesy of the National Archives*

Capt. Richard Gales, deputy commander of a supply convoy on the Ledo Road, giving a child a ride on his WLA at the Tengchung Cutoff, China-Burma border, March 1945. *Courtesy of the National Archives*

Sgt. Oliver Lincoln, Cpl. Erwin Mueller, and Sgt. Philip McConkey of the 4th Marine Division repair a captured Rikuo on Iwo Jima in February 1945. *Courtesy of the National Archives*

CHAPTER 6
The WLA in the Red Army

The WLA served in the largest numbers and in the most-significant roles in the Soviet armed forces. The Soviet Union received 27,100 WLAs under the Lend-Lease program, making it the leading user of the WLA during the war, with more of them than the US armed forces. Moreover, in the Red Army the WLA was a combat vehicle, performing the reconnaissance role once considered for it by the US Army. Red Army motorcyclists would ride the WLA deep behind enemy lines, leading offensive operations in advance of their tank armies. They would do so all the way to Berlin.

Before the German invasion of the Soviet Union in June 1941, a motorcycle regiment was the primary reconnaissance force of each Red Army armored formation. The Red Army was creating an armored force of twenty-nine mechanized corps in 1941, with nine already formed by January 1941 and twenty more beginning to form in February 1941. Each mechanized corps was to have over 37,000 men and 1,000 tanks, with two tank divisions, a mechanized infantry division, a motorcycle regiment, a signals battalion, an engineer battalion, and an aviation troop. The motorcycle regiment was the reconnaissance unit of the mechanized corps. Each was actually a large battalion with over 600 men, lightly armed with infantry weapons: rifles, submachine guns, light machine guns, and mortars. At least twenty-seven motorcycle regiments had formed by June 22, 1941.[1]

The motorcycles were sidecar outfits that served as transports for three-man scout teams. They were intended to be the M72, a Soviet copy of the BMW R71, a civilian model produced from 1938 to 1941 that had also been the basis for the Harley-Davidson XA. A large motorcycle with a side-valve 750 cc engine, telescopic front forks, and plunger rear suspension, it had seats for two soldiers and a sidecar carrying a third soldier with a mounting point for a Degtyarev DP-28 machine gun, the standard light

machine gun of the Red Army. M72 production began in a factory in Moscow in early 1941.[2]

The German invasion that commenced on June 22, 1941, caught the Soviet Union by surprise and rapidly accomplished the almost complete destruction of the Red Army. The Red Army's losses in 1941 equaled or exceeded its strength of 4.5 million in June 1941, and it had to abandon its prewar organization as its units were destroyed and raw units of new draftees took their place. The mechanized corps all were destroyed or disbanded and ceased to exist. Reduced to hastily formed infantry divisions and tank battalions and brigades, the Red Army would have to start

A motorcycle regiment, with three-man teams on sidecar-equipped M72 motorcycles, moving through Moscow to the front line defending against the German offensive toward the city in October 1941. *Author's collection*

over to make itself into a modern army capable of fighting the German invaders.

The Red Army rebounded from the defeats of 1941 by radically revising its organization and tactics. In March 1942, drawing on lessons learned in battle, the Red Army began the formation of larger tank units. Its new tank corps were small armored divisions, which began with two to three tank brigades and a motorized rifle brigade, then added supporting units to make them into complete combined arms teams. By July 1942, each tank corps included a battalion of truck-mounted Katyusha rocket launchers for artillery support, a motorcycle battalion, an engineer company, an antiaircraft battalion, and maintenance and supply units. The organization of multiple tank corps into tank armies began in May 1942. Mechanized corps, each with three mechanized infantry brigades and a tank brigade, also began to form in September 1942. By January 1943, the Red Army had formed two tank armies, twenty-four tank corps, and eight mechanized corps. These formations were in addition to numerous independent tank brigades, regiments, and battalions for infantry support.

The United States made a crucial contribution to equipping the rebuilt Red Army. Under the Lend-Lease program and direct contracts with US companies, the Soviet Union received enormous quantities of equipment and supplies from the United States: 14,203 aircraft, including 9,438 fighters, 3,771 bombers, and 708 transport planes; 6,196 tanks and 4,158 other armored vehicles; 43,728 Jeeps and 3,510 amphibious Jeeps; 363,080 trucks; 11,075 railroad cars; 380,000 field telephones; four million tons of metals; and five million tons of food.[3] American-made vehicles made an especially crucial contribution to the Red Army's ability to fight the German forces on an equal footing. With the Soviet Union lacking the automobile industry necessary to produce large numbers of trucks and other vehicles, the US automobile industry provided them instead.

American-made motorcycles took the place of machines that the Soviet Union lacked the capacity to produce. Under Lend-Lease, 32,200 motorcycles from Harley-Davidson and Indian went to the Soviet Union.[4] A total of 27,100 of these were WLAs, the remainder being Indians. British-made motorcycles, primarily from BSA and Velocette, also went to the Soviet Union as military aid. Soviet industry produced only 9,799 of the M72 during the war, in a factory relocated from Moscow to the town of Irbit in the Ural Mountains. The WLA became the primary vehicle of the Red Army's motorcycle battalions, outnumbering all other types put together by a factor of two to one.

Lend-Lease Indian 741B with Soviet-made rear seat, sidecar, and Degtyarev DP-28 machine gun, in 1943. *Author's collection*

The WLA and the Red Army's motorcycle battalions proved to be a perfect match of vehicle and mission. The WLA, with its 750 cc engine and large frame by European standards, was well suited to substitute for the M72 in the Red Army's tactical concept of the motorcycle as a carrier for a three-man scout team. The Red Army equipped its WLAs with the rear seat and sidecar from the M72, to perform the same role in the motorcycle battalions. The proven and reliable design of the WLA, which ran well on Soviet low-octane gas with its low 5:1 compression ratio and rarely broke down, made it even more suitable. The Red Army used their Indians, which were primarily the 750 cc 741B, similarly in some motorcycle units, but they considered their Indians to be less reliable than the WLA. British motorcycles, with their smaller engines and frames, were too small to be suitable for the role filled by the WLA in the motorcycle battalions.

The motorcycle battalions formed in 1942 were lightly armed formations similar to the motorcycle regiments of 1941. Under the organization adopted in May 1942, they had large quantities of automatic weapons but no armored vehicles or heavy weapons. Each battalion had two motorcycle companies of seventy-four men, each with twenty-one motorcycles and armed entirely with automatic weapons: twenty-four light machine guns, and twenty-six submachine guns. Each battalion also had a rifle company of sixty-one men with eight light machine guns and sixteen submachine guns. A mortar platoon with four 82 mm mortars provided its

Motorcycle troops on an Indian 741B display their primary weapons, the Degtyarev DP-28 light machine gun and PPSh-41 submachine gun. *Author's collection*

only fire support.[5] These battalions had the mobility to scout ahead of the Red Army's tank and infantry units, but with no armored vehicles or artillery, they lacked the firepower to punch through enemy forces when they made contact.

The rapid expansion of the Red Army's tank and mechanized corps and the availability of Lend-Lease WLAs and Indians led to the formation of a large number of new motorcycle battalions. In February 1943, the Red Army had created at least twenty-two motorcycle battalions, and by the end of 1943, there were at least forty-one.[6] In addition, some of the twenty-seven motorcycle regiments of 1941 survived the defeats of 1941–42, with at least eight continuing into and beyond 1943.[7] They reorganized following the format of the new motorcycle battalions.

Armored car battalions were initially the reconnaissance units of the mechanized corps when they began to form in September 1942. An armored car battalion had two armored car companies with five armored cars each. In April 1943, each armored car company acquired a motorcycle platoon of seven motorcycles with seven light machine guns and a rifle platoon with four light machine guns.[8] Like the motorcycle battalions, the armored car battalions were lightly armed and capable of scouting but not of any significant combat.

In addition to the motorcycle and armored car battalions, tank and mechanized corps had reconnaissance units with motorcycles in many of their component units. Tank brigades had a platoon of three armored cars and a motorcycle platoon in 1941, dropping the motorcycle platoon in 1942.[9] The motorized rifle brigades in tank corps each had a reconnaissance company with an armored car platoon, a motorcycle platoon, and a truck-mounted rifle platoon in 1942, replaced in October 1943 with an armored car platoon, a rifle platoon in ten armored personnel carriers, and two truck-mounted infantry platoons.[10] Mechanized brigades had a reconnaissance company identical to those of motorized rifle brigades in 1942, replaced in April 1944 with a company consisting of an armored car platoon, a motorcycle platoon of three motorcycles, and a rifle platoon in ten armored personnel carriers.[11]

A more heavily armed motorcycle battalion adopted in November 1943 replaced both the motorcycle battalion of the tank corps and the armored car battalion of the mechanized corps, providing each formation with a reconnaissance unit that was a more powerful combined-arms team. Each battalion now had a tank company with ten medium tanks, two motorcycle companies with the same strength as in 1942, a rifle company with ten armored personnel carriers, a battery of antitank guns, and a mortar platoon with four 82 mm mortars.[12] With tanks, armored infantry, antitank

WLAs of the 4th Motorcycle Regiment, part of the 6th Tank Army, in Romania in August 1944. They are passing a column of US-made M3 half-tracks with a 57 mm antitank gun, called the T48 by the US Army and the SU-57 by the Red Army. *Author's collection*

The equipment of the reorganized and rearmed motorcycle battalions varied considerably from unit to unit, making heavy use of US-made vehicles provided under Lend-Lease. Most would have used the WLA as their primary motorcycle, with some using the M72 or the Indian 741B. The medium tanks ideally would have been T-34s, but they could have been Lend-Lease M4 Sherman medium tanks or any other American or British tank provided to the Soviet Union. The rifle company could have American M3 or M5 half-tracks, M3A1 Scout Cars, or British Bren Carriers as armored personnel carriers, or only unarmored trucks or Jeeps. Similarly, the antitank guns normally would be the Soviet ZIS-3 76.2 mm divisional gun, a superb artillery piece used both for indirect fire and as an antitank gun, but could be American or British.

The motorcycle battalion as organized and equipped in late 1943 lasted to the end of the war in May 1945. These units led the exploitation of breakthroughs by Soviet tank armies and tank and mechanized corps in all major offensives in 1944 and 1945. They provided the same capability that the US Army had sought in its experiments with mechanized cavalry in 1940–41, using mostly the same American-made vehicles: the WLA, half-tracks, scout cars, and Jeeps. In these units, soldiers on WLAs led the forces of the Red Army westward all the way to Berlin.

artillery, and direct and indirect fire support, these new motorcycle battalions had both the mobility to scout in advance of tank and mechanized units and the armor and firepower to attack retreating enemy units and to overpower defenses, to seize and secure important terrain such as river crossings and road junctions.

Close-up of T48/SU-57 half-track self-propelled 57 mm antitank guns with a passing WLA. *Author's collection*

Mortars and WLAs of a motorcycle battalion at Baranovichi, Poland, in July 1944. *Author's collection*

87th Guards Motorcycle Battalion

The 87th Guards Motorcycle Battalion began as one of the motorcycle battalions newly formed in early 1943, and in two years of combat it fought in many of the Red Army's most significant battles from Kursk to the fall of Berlin.

The battalion formed in Moscow from March 8 to May 28, 1943, as the 87th Motorcycle Battalion, and in the following year it participated in several of the largest battles on the Eastern Front. Assigned to the 2nd Tank Army as part of the operational reserve of the Central Front, holding the northern side of the Kursk salient, the battalion received its baptism of fire during the Battle of Kursk. When the German offensive began on July 5, the battalion participated in the defense against the northern arm of the German pincer movement at the key town of Ponyri, which defeated the German advance after the commitment of the 2nd Tank Army on July 6. It then participated in the counter-offensive that drove back German forces to the north of Kursk and liberated the city of Orel on August 5.

Withdrawn from combat for rest and refitting with the 2nd Tank Army in September 1943, the battalion reorganized and reequipped following the new 1943 pattern for motorcycle battalions. The battalion received its company of medium tanks on January 10, 1944, then fought in its first battle with its new organization and weapons only a few days later. Reassigned along with the 2nd Tank Army to the 1st Ukrainian Front on January 18, 1944, the battalion participated in the battle outside the Korsun pocket in January–February 1944, one of the largest encirclements of German forces by the Red Army between the Battle of Stalingrad in February 1943 and the Soviet summer offensive that began in July 1944.

The unit proved the effectiveness of the new motorcycle battalion as a reconnaissance unit during the offensive from Ukraine into Romania in the spring of 1944. With the German front in Ukraine broken after the battles during the preceding months, the 2nd Tank Army in mid-March sent the battalion ahead deep into German-held territory to secure a crossing over the Dniester River at the town of Yampil. Moving over 150 kilometers in two days from March 15 to 17, the battalion cleared the town of German defenders and secured the crossing, establishing a bridgehead across the Dniester for the 2nd Tank Army to exploit. It then crossed into Romanian territory, scouting toward the city of Iasi until June 1944.

Transferred north to Belarus for the 1944 summer offensive, as part of the 1st Belorussian Front, the battalion led the 2nd Tank Army's drive deep into German-held Poland, which began on July 18. The offensive liberated the Polish city of Lublin on July 24 and reached the outskirts of Warsaw during the first week of August. For its successful role in the offensive, the 2nd Tank Army and the 87th Motorcycle Battalion received the honorific "Guards" designation in November 1944, the motorcycle unit becoming the 87th Guards Motorcycle Battalion.

In the Red Army's winter 1945 offensive, which began on January 12, the 87th Guards Motorcycle Battalion and the 2nd Guards Tank Army advanced 700 kilometers from just south of Warsaw to the Oder River, only 70 kilometers from Berlin, in only fifteen days. They then turned north to invade Pomerania, then part of Germany and now in Poland, to secure the Red Army's right flank before the drive to Berlin. The battalion was the first Red Army unit to enter Pomerania on January 27, and reached the Baltic Sea within a week.

In the Battle of Berlin, which ended the war in Europe, the 87th Guards Motorcycle Battalion led the 2nd Guards Tank Army's advance to Berlin as the northern arm of the pincer movement that surrounded the city. After the Red Army broke through German defenses along the Oder River in April 16–19, the battalion led the 2nd Guards Tank Army's advance to the north of Berlin, which culminated in the 2nd Guards Tank Army linking up with Red Army forces advancing from the southeast on April 24. The battalion and other 2nd Guards Tank Army units secured the encirclement of Berlin while other units besieged the city and ended the battle and the war in Europe on May 2.

After the war, the 87th Guards Motorcycle Battalion became based in the Carpathian military district in western Ukraine. It continues in the army of Ukraine as the 54th Guards Reconnaissance Battalion, which inherited the lineage and battle honors of the wartime unit.[13]

CHAPTER 7
The WLA in Other Allied Armies

Additional Allied armies used the WLA and other US-made military motorcycles during the war. Over 7,000 WLAs and 20,000 other Harley-Davidsons went to countries other than the United States and the Soviet Union, and the majority of Indian's wartime production of 42,044 military motorcycles was exported as direct sales to foreign militaries or under Lend-Lease.[1] These motorcycles performed important roles in many Allied armies in Europe, Africa, and Asia.

Canada

As a nation within the British Commonwealth, Canada organized its armed forces following British lines and used British equipment, and its forces fought under British command. Its use of British equipment included motorcycles, which before the war were primarily British-made machines by BSA, Norton, and Triumph. Britain's shortages of military equipment forced Canada to look for alternative sources for many types of equipment, however, and motorcycles were among them. Canada turned to the United States, becoming one of the largest users of US-made motorcycles during the war.

Indian was the first US supplier of motorcycles to the Canadian National Defense Forces. In 1940, Canada received 150 Indian Chiefs originally ordered by France, whose contract with Indian had been taken over by Britain after the fall of France. Canada placed additional orders with Indian for Chiefs and 640 Scouts, but Indian had difficulty meeting the orders. As a result, Canada turned to Harley-Davidson to supply its armed forces with motorcycles.

Harley-Davidson developed the Model WLC ("C" for Canada) in response to Canada's request. The WLC was based on the WLA and was largely unchanged in its major mechanical systems, but it incorporated detail changes that made it more compatible with British riding practices. The WLC used a British-style hand clutch lever instead of the WLA's foot clutch pedal, although it retained the hand gearshift of the WLA instead of using a British-style foot shift. It also had a front stand, in addition to the WLA's rear stand, and changes to other details.

The Canadian armed forces received 18,020 WLCs from 1941 through 1944, 77 percent of the number of WLAs delivered to the much-larger US armed forces, and 20 percent of Harley-Davidson's total production of military motorcycles during the war.

United Kingdom

The United Kingdom was the largest user of motorcycles among the Allied powers, acquiring over 425,000—over ten times the number acquired by the larger US armed forces during the war. The British army, Royal Navy, Royal Air Force, and Home Guard all used substantial numbers of motorcycles, to provide transportation for dispatch riders, military police, and others. Lacking their own equivalent of the Jeep, and receiving only limited numbers of them through Lend-Lease, the United Kingdom continued to use motorcycles for many roles filled by Jeeps in the US armed forces. The British armed forces relied primarily on their own domestic motorcycle industry, purchasing various models from multiple companies. BSA, the largest British motorcycle manufacturer, produced over 126,000 of a single model, the M20. Norton made over 76,000 of the 16H; Triumph, 49,700 machines of various types; Matchless, over 52,000 G3/Ls; and Ariel, over 40,000 of its W/NG.[2]

Heavy losses during German victories in 1940–41 and damage inflicted on British war industry by German bombing forced the United Kingdom to turn to the United States for additional machines. The evacuation of the British Expeditionary Force at Dunkirk alone cost the British army approximately 700 tanks,

880 field guns, 310 heavy artillery pieces, 500 antiaircraft guns, 850 antitank guns, 11,000 machine guns, 45,000 trucks and cars, and 20,000 motorcycles. Bombings of the city of Coventry by the German Blitz from September to November 1940 worsened the situation by destroying the Triumph motorcycle factory, Britain's second largest after BSA's. Britain lost Triumph's production capacity from November 1940 until a new Triumph factory opened in 1942. These compounding pressures led the British War Department to place orders both with Harley-Davidson and Indian in 1940–41.

During the fall of France in 1940, the United Kingdom took over an order by France for Indian Chiefs. On June 17, 1940, hours before the French government under Marshal Henri Petain asked Germany for an armistice, the United Kingdom signed contracts transferring French orders for US-produced military equipment to the UK, including a partially completed order for 5,000 of the Chief-derived Indian 340B. The United Kingdom received 325 Indian 340Bs in July–August 1940.[3]

The United Kingdom ordered additional motorcycles from Harley-Davidson and Indian starting in 1941. The British army and the Royal Air Force received an unknown number of the Harley-Davidson WLC in 1942–43. They also received large numbers of Indians, starting with 236 340B sidecar machines in 1941–42 and 7,550 741B solo motorcycles in 1942–43. The Ministry of War Transport received a further fifty Indian 741Bs.[4] The United Kingdom also received 360 examples of the 344B, a 1,204 cc side-valve motorcycle with a sidecar, in 1944.[5]

The United Kingdom also provided US-made motorcycles to Commonwealth countries and to Allied forces in exile that fought under British command. These uses are addressed under each country.

Australia

Australian troops fought under British command and used British army organization and equipment, and, like Canada, Australia turned to the United States to supply motorcycles and other motor vehicles. Australia received 4,200 WLAs under Lend-Lease. Additionally, under a joint contract with South Africa in 1944, Australia obtained 100 74-cubic-inch Model US motorcycles and fifty of the Model WS, a version of the Forty-Five with a low compression engine and sidecar gearing. Through UK contracts, Australia also received 4,158 of the Indian 741B.[6] These deliveries made Australia the fourth-largest user of the WLA and WLC during the war, after the United States, the Soviet Union, and Canada, and the fifth-largest user of US-made motorcycles, after those countries and the United Kingdom.

New Zealand

The armed forces of New Zealand, organized and equipped similarly to those of Australia and serving in the same theaters, also used quantities of US-made motorcycles as substitutes for British equipment that was not available. New Zealand received 3,616 of the Indian 741B through UK contracts.[7]

South Africa

Similar to Canada, Australia, and New Zealand, South Africa used British army organization and equipment but was unable to obtain motorcycles in sufficient numbers from the United Kingdom and therefore turned to the United States. South Africa used both Forty-Five-based and "big twin" 74-cubic-inch Model US machines from Harley-Davidson, along with a small number of the Indian 741B.

The Forty-Five model made for South Africa was a Model WL, which lacked many of the modifications added to the WLA's. Its engine had the older iron cylinder heads instead of the WLA's aluminum cylinder heads, a civilian-style air cleaner rather than the WLA's specialized military air cleaner, and other features from previous Forty-Fives. South Africa obtained 2,350 of these WLs in 1941 under a direct contract with Harley-Davidson.

Other Harley-Davidson and Indian motorcycles came to South Africa under various direct contracts with the manufacturers and Lend-Lease contracts. Approximately 1,800 of the Harley-Davidson Model US were used by the South African Army and Maritime Forces. The South African Maritime Forces also received seventy-two Indian 741Bs from a UK contract.[8]

Republic of China

The Republic of China, also called Nationalist China, received support from the United States under Lend-Lease for its defense against the Japanese invasion, which had begun in 1937. China, along with the United Kingdom, had been one of the original intended recipients of assistance under the Lend-Lease program when it was signed into law in March 1941. Military equipment supplied to China under Lend-Lease included 1,000 WLAs.

In addition to WLAs provided under Lend-Lease, China may have used Harley-Davidson copies produced in Imperial Japan by Rikuo. The Rikuo was a copy of the side-valve-engine Harley-Davidson Model VL, a design dating back to the early 1930s. During their eight-year-long war against the Japanese invasion from 1937 to 1945, Chinese forces may have captured substantial numbers of Rikuos from the Japanese forces and put them into service against their original users.

India

The Indian Army, which fought in North Africa, Europe, and Asia and had over 2.5 million men by the end of the Second World War, used British military organization and equipment, including some US-made motorcycles. The Indian army received 1,000 of the Indian 741B from UK contracts.[9]

Poland

After the fall of Poland in September 1939, Poles who had escaped the German invasion fought under the command of the United Kingdom and the Soviet Union. The two Polish exile forces existed completely separately, divided by the political differences between the Western allies and the Soviet Union and organized and equipped following different foreign models.

Polish forces in exile in the West first formed in France and then re-formed in the UK after the fall of France in 1940. By the end of the war, there were 195,000 men in the Polish armed forces in the West under British command, in units that included three infantry divisions, two armored divisions, two independent armored brigades, and a parachute brigade. Their organization followed British army models, and they received British army arms and equipment. Their vehicles included US-made motorcycles from British army contracts, twelve Indian 340Bs, and 683 Indian 741Bs.[10]

The Soviet Union, which had invaded Poland in September 1939 and held tens of thousands of Polish prisoners of war from 1939 to 1941, released many of them and formed a Polish military force under Soviet command in response to the German invasion in June 1941. Polish forces in the East grew by the end of the war to the 1st Polish Army, which fought in Belarus, Poland, and the Battle of Berlin in 1943–45; the 2nd Polish Army, which fought in Germany south of Berlin and in the liberation of Prague in 1945; and a Polish air force with bombers, ground attack aircraft, and fighters. With ten infantry divisions, a tank corps, and numerous supporting tank, artillery, antitank, antiaircraft, and engineer units, these forces had units that would have used the WLA, the Indian 741B, or the Soviet-made M72 in substantial numbers. They included the 1st Motorcycle Battalion, the reconnaissance unit of the 1st Polish Army, and the 1st Tank Corps, part of the 2nd Polish Army.[11]

France

France was the first Allied country to order American motorcycles for its armed forces. In October 1939, shortly after the German invasion of Poland in September 1939, France placed an order for 5,000 of the Indian 340B.[12] Indian had 2,200 of these machines ready for delivery by March 1940, but the freighter shipping them from New York to France in April disappeared without a trace, presumably torpedoed and sunk by a German U-boat.[13] With the fall of France in June 1940, the United Kingdom took over the remainder of the order.

The Free French Forces under General Charles de Gaulle used US tanks and other US-made vehicles, including WLA motorcycles. The Free French received 589 WLAs. These motorcycles equipped the 1st Free French Division, which fought in North Africa, Italy, southern France, Alsace, and Germany; the 2nd French Armored Division, which landed in Normandy after D-day, liberated Paris and led de Gaulle's parade through the city, liberated Strasbourg, and participated in the invasion of Germany; and other units of the Free French Forces.

Brazil

Brazil was the smallest Allied user of the WLA during the Second World War, receiving 430 WLAs.

Iran

The Imperial State of Iran became one of the Allied powers in 1943. The Soviet Union and the United Kingdom invaded Iran in August–September 1941 in order to secure a supply line for Lend-Lease aid, resulting in the abdication of Reza Shah Pahlavi and the accession of Mohammad Reza Shah Pahlavi, who became the last shah of Iran. Iran officially declared war on Germany in September 1943.

Iran obtained an undetermined number of Indian 741Bs in early 1944. These motorcycles equipped the Imperial Iranian Gendarmerie, whose motorcycle school graduated its first motorcyclists in March 1944.

New Zealand military policeman Lance Cpl. M. E. Middlemiss with an Indian 741B in New Caledonia in February 1944. *Courtesy of the National Archives*

Motorcyclist of the army of the Republic of China crossing a stream. *Courtesy of the National Archives*

Free French military police riding WLAs, escorting a car carrying Charles de Gaulle through the town of Maiche, near the border between France and Germany, in September 1944. *Courtesy of the National Archives*

Imperial Iranian Gendarmerie with Indian 741Bs at their Central Headquarters in Tehran in December 1944. *Courtesy of the National Archives*

Stunt-riding demonstration on Indian 741Bs at the graduation ceremony of Imperial Iranian Gendarmerie on March 27, 1944. The graduates received their certificates from Col. (later major general) Norman Schwarzkopf Sr., father of Gen. Norman Schwarzkopf Jr., commander of Coalition forces in Operation Desert Storm. *Courtesy of the National Archives*

CHAPTER 8
The WLA after the War

The end of the Second World War meant the end of US and foreign military use of the WLA on a large scale. The rapid return to the United States of US military units from Europe after V-E Day and from Asia after V-J Day resulted in vast quantities of vehicles and other military equipment being left overseas, no longer needed with the organizations and people who had used them being demobilized by the millions. The unneeded vehicles, discarded in vast dumps full of surplus military equipment, included thousands of WLAs. The Army and Marine Corps had already largely eliminated them from their official unit organizations, and those that remained were left behind when the soldiers and Marines who had kept them went home.

Small numbers of motorcycles remained in service with US military police in Germany and Japan and at other US military posts around the world. The WLA quickly became obsolete after the war, however, and it lasted in US military service into the 1950s but then was replaced. Overhead-valve engines and rear suspension, which had been advanced features in prewar American motorcycles but that the WLA did not have, soon became normal in civilian motorcycles. Harley-Davidson replaced its prewar WL series with

Corporal Chad Conway and Corporal Doubfit, motorcyclists of the 82nd Military Police Platoon, 82nd Airborne Division, in Berlin in May 1945. *Courtesy of the US Army Military Police Corps Regimental Museum*

Cpl. Chad Conway of the 82nd Military Police Platoon, 82nd Airborne Division, with division commander General James Gavin's escort in September 1945. *Courtesy of the US Army Military Police Corps Regimental Museum*

Sgt. Gene Stephens of the 281st Military Police Company in Rome, holding a newspaper with a headline celebrating the end of the war. His WLA has civilian-style brightwork instead of military olive drab on many of its parts. *Courtesy of the US Army Military Police Corps Regimental Museum*

Discarded WLAs in the vast US Army surplus vehicle park at Mourmelon Le Grand, France, near Reims, in February 1946. *Courtesy of the National Archives*

the Model K with rear suspension in 1952, and then with the XL Sportster with an overhead-valve engine in 1957. As a result, the Army acquired small numbers of additional WLAs from 1949 through 1952, mostly in 1952 as the US rearmed for the Korean War, but in 1957 placed an order for a military version of the XL Sportster called the XLA. The more modern XLA replaced the WLA in the limited roles for motorcycles in the Army.

Another view of the US Army surplus vehicle park at Mourmelon Le Grand in February 1946. *Courtesy of the National Archives*

XLA at the Golden Gate Bridge. Note the rectangular oil bath air cleaner, similar to the unit on the WLA. *Courtesy of the US Army Military Police Corps Regimental Museum*

Sgt. First Class Beecher Dyke, 6th Cavalry Regiment/Group

Beecher Dyke served as a horse cavalryman and as a motorcyclist in the mechanized cavalry prior to the US entering the Second World War, fought in and survived the war in Europe, and after the war became an Army motorcyclist again in the military police.

Born in the mountains of eastern Tennessee in April 1919, Dyke grew up in rural poverty during the Depression in a family with ten children, and he enlisted in the Army to escape life as a farmhand working for fifty cents a day. Enlisting in August 1939 at Fort Oglethorpe, Georgia, the base of the Regular Army's 6th Cavalry Regiment, he became a cavalry trooper in the 6th Cavalry and remained one for the duration of the war.

In his prewar service, Dyke experienced the end of the era of horse cavalry and participated in the Army's brief experiment with motorcycles as a cavalry fighting vehicle. Like all cavalrymen, he loved his horse, named Smokey, and was sad when the Army took away the troop's horses and issued motorcycles in their place. The 6th Cavalry received a mix of Harley-Davidsons and Indians, with Dyke favoring the Indian, finding it to be faster and preferring its left-hand throttle, being left-handed. Their riding gear included the gold-colored leather helmets, later taken away and reissued to tank crews. Their experimental maneuvers on the Civil War battlefield of Chickamauga lasted from December 1939 to late 1941, ending shortly before the attack on Pearl Harbor.

When the 6th Cavalry went to war, it would do so in armored vehicles and Jeeps rather than motorcycles, and it would perform a unique role in the advance of Gen. George S. Patton's 3rd Army across Europe. The 6th Cavalry embarked for Europe in October 1943 onboard the ocean liner *Queen Elizabeth*, and it trained in the United Kingdom until July 1944, reorganized and redesignated as the 6th Cavalry Group in January 1944. The unit landed at Utah

Beecher Dyke. *Courtesy of Jack Dyke*

Beach on July 10, 1944, and became an element of Patton's Third Army. Patton gave the 6th Cavalry a special mission as his Army Information Service, with the task of keeping the Third Army command informed of the location and disposition of friendly and German units at the quickly moving front. This role led to the unit nickname "Patton's Household Cavalry." In November, when the Third Army encountered rough terrain and autumn and

Beecher Dyke (*right*) as a military policeman in Germany after the war. *Courtesy of Jack Dyke*

winter weather that slowed its operations, the 6th Cavalry reorganized as a combined-arms task force with an attached Ranger infantry battalion, tank destroyers, and combat engineers.

Dyke was nearly killed in action in the Battle of the Bulge in December 1944, riding one of the Jeeps that had replaced the 6th Cavalry's motorcycles. At the beginning of Patton's offensive to relieve the besieged 101st Airborne Division in Bastogne, in which the 6th Cavalry protected the right flank of the 4th Armored Division, Dyke was the point man, riding in a Jeep leading a force toward a German-held town. Following standard cavalry reconnaissance tactics, Dyke rode in a Jeep with a machine gun at the head of the vehicle column, followed by an M8 armored car with a 37 mm antitank gun and machine guns and by a Jeep carrying a mortar. In the event of contact, the crew of the lead Jeep would make a U-turn quickly, or bail out and take cover—a perilous task, which Dyke had done many times—while the armored car and mortar provided direct and indirect fire support. Dyke's Jeep crossed a bridge and arrived at a turn in the road at the same time as a German column arriving from the other side, and the Germans opened fire first. Three bullets from a submachine gun hit Dyke, and his patrol fell back, leaving him behind. Dyke crawled back to the bridge and floated across the river to the other side before passing out. The unit's first sergeant, finding that Dyke was missing, went back to

Beecher Dyke's military police motorcycle unit. *Courtesy of Jack Dyke*

Beecher Dyke at a checkpoint with a German policeman. *Courtesy of Jack Dyke*

the bridge and found him. Evacuated and sent to a hospital, Dyke recovered from his wounds and returned to action only a month later.

In 1945, reunited with the 6th Cavalry, Dyke participated in the invasion and occupation of Germany. He took part in breaching the Siegfried Line guarding Germany's western border in February–March, crossing the Rhine River in March, and the subsequent drive across Germany. In mid-April, the 6th Cavalry overran a concentration camp at Ohrdruf, where the SS guards had evacuated prisoners able to walk and shot the remainder, leaving the bodies in a pile, with other bodies stacked around an incinerator. As the Third Army moved south into Bavaria to clear out German forces rumored to be preparing a last stand in the Alps, the 6th Cavalry guarded the 3rd Army's lengthening left flank. The 6th Cavalry continued to push eastward until Germany surrendered, ending the war across the border between Germany and Czechoslovakia. The unit then settled into occupation duty in Germany.

Dyke received five Bronze Star awards for courage under fire and a Purple Heart for his wounds during the Battle of the Bulge.

After the end of the war, Dyke briefly left the Army but soon reenlisted and served until 1960. Dyke mustered out with an honorable discharge at Camp Atterbury, Indiana, on September 9, 1945. Just over two months later, he reenlisted on November 20, 1945. He ended up back on motorcycles with the military police, then became a tank crewman during the 1950s. Serving in Germany and Austria, he became a pioneering American motorcyclist in another way, becoming one of the first to tour Europe by motorcycle. His travels took him all over Germany, Austria, and other countries in Europe, including to Hitler's Eagles Nest in Berchtesgaden.

Dyke married his wife, Evelyn, in Ringgold, Georgia, a town near Chattanooga, Tennessee, on November 22, 1948. He and Evelyn had four children, whom they raised in Germany, Chicago, and northern Georgia. They settled down in northern Georgia and lived there for the rest of his life.

Beecher Dyke passed away on March 26, 2007, at the age of eighty-seven. He is buried in Chattanooga National Cemetery in Chattanooga, Tennessee, near the eastern Tennessee mountains where he was born and the Chickamauga battlefield where he once rode horses and motorcycles with the 6th Cavalry.

In the Soviet Union, the Red Army replaced its WLAs soon after the war. Shipments of US-made motorcycles and spare parts under Lend-Lease ended with V-E Day, with numerous undelivered or incomplete machines kept in the United States. The BMW-based M72 continued in full-scale production after the war, again becoming the Red Army's standard military motorcycle. The M72 replaced the WLA and other American and British motorcycles in the Red Army. The M72 design also served as the basis for civilian motorcycle production in the Soviet Union, as the Ural in Russia and the Dnepr in Ukraine.

Some war-surplus WLAs and WLCs went back into military use in the armies of new countries. For example, Greece used WLAs and WLCs in its re-created army after its liberation from Axis occupation in 1945.

A second life for the WLA began immediately after the war, however, as civilians in Europe took WLAs and other discarded Allied military motorcycles and used them as personal transportation. Large numbers of WLAs, WLCs, Indians, and British motorcycles no longer needed by the demobilizing armies of the United States and the other Western Allied nations ended up in the hands of civilians in need of transportation. With Europe deprived and stripped of civilian motor vehicles during the war, and the continent's industries largely in ruins, surplus military vehicles such as the WLA filled a vital need for people struggling to rebuild their lives. In the Soviet Union, where the Red Army was replacing its WLAs with the domestic M72, the WLA also left military service and became a civilian vehicle. The WLA and its counterparts became basic transportation for ordinary people across Europe.

Private Sessler of the 545th Military Police Company, 1st Cavalry Division, passes Japanese civilians. *Courtesy of the US Army Military Police Corps Regimental Museum*

Motorcyclists of the 1st Infantry Division military police platoon in Germany in 1948. Note the front wheel spats and other peacetime decorative details. *Courtesy of the US Army Military Police Corps Regimental Museum*

82nd Airborne Division military police platoon motorcycle team. *Courtesy of the US Army Military Police Corps Regimental Museum*

Military police patrol circa 1949. *Courtesy of the US Army Military Police Corps Regimental Museum*

WLAs of the 759th Military Police Battalion at Berlin's Brandenburg Gate. *Courtesy of the US Army Military Police Corps Regimental Museum*

Sergeant Ralph Campbell, Company B, 709th Military Police Battalion, in Frankfurt, Germany, with the first military police motorcycle with a two-way radio in Europe, in 1950. *Courtesy of the US Army Military Police Corps Regimental Museum*

Military police WLAs in Augsberg, Germany. *Courtesy of the US Army Military Police Corps Regimental Museum*

Military police on WLAs escorting M24 light tanks on parade in Germany. *Courtesy of the US Army Military Police Corps Regimental Museum*

Motorcycle patrol of the 720th Military Police Battalion at Camp Burness, Tokyo, Japan, in September 1949. *Courtesy of the US Army Military Police Corps Regimental Museum*

Private Sessler of the 545th Military Police Company, 1st Cavalry Division, on base on the island of Hokkaido, Japan, in 1954. *Courtesy of the US Army Military Police Corps Regimental Museum*

Private Sessler of the 545th Military Police Company, 1st Cavalry Division. *Courtesy of the US Army Military Police Corps Regimental Museum*

760th Military Police Battalion with WLAs in the Panama Canal Zone in 1948. *Courtesy of the US Army Military Police Corps Regimental Museum*

760th Military Police Battalion with WLAs in the Panama Canal Zone in 1948. *Courtesy of the US Army Military Police Corps Regimental Museum*

WLAs of the 760th Military Police Battalion in the Panama Canal Zone, lined up for inspection. *Courtesy of the US Army Military Police Corps Regimental Museum*

In the United States, where new cars and motorcycles were plentiful, the WLA became a cheap surplus machine. Many became customized as "bobbers" or "choppers," losing their military origins as parts were removed, frames were altered, and many machines were ridden to destruction or wrecked in accidents.

Decades after the end of the war, a movement toward restoration and preservation of surviving WLAs began and spread throughout the United States and Europe. Interest in the history of the WLA was especially strong in continental Europe, where large numbers had remained after the war, and many people associated the WLA with liberation from Nazi Germany. An indication of the leading role of continental Europe in the revival of interest in the WLA is that the widely used nickname "Liberator" first emerged in Belgium, not in the United States or elsewhere in the English-speaking world.

During the 1990s, the restoration and preservation of WLAs advanced significantly as collectors rediscovered large numbers of machines. The fall of the Berlin Wall in 1989 and the collapse of the Soviet Union in 1991 led to the discovery of thousands of WLAs sent to the Soviet Union under Lend-Lease, long hidden behind the Iron Curtain. Russia and other former Soviet and Warsaw Pact states have become leading sources of surviving WLAs for restoration.

How the US armed forces and other Allied armies actually used the WLA during the Second World War remained unclear for many years, however, obscured by generalizations about its use in the United States and lack of knowledge about its service in the Soviet Union. Information now available in the United States, Russia, and other countries makes it clear that the WLA and other US-made motorcycles served in all major Allied armies, from countries on six continents, and served on every battlefront of the war in Europe, North Africa, and Asia. Moreover, they were frontline combat vehicles for many Allied soldiers, particularly those of the Red Army. Now it is apparent that although the story of the WLA began in the United States, during the war it became a worldwide story.

Each WLA, WLC, Indian, and other military motorcycle that has survived is a memorial to the Allied cause in the country in which it served. With more surviving to be restored and preserved with each passing decade, the future of this heritage appears to be secure.

WLAs of the 760th Military Police Battalion in the Panama Canal Zone, lined up for inspection. *Courtesy of the US Army Military Police Corps Regimental Museum*

WLA of the 549th Military Police
Company in Fort Amador, Panama
Canal Zone. *Courtesy of the US
Army Military Police Corps
Regimental Museum*

WLA of the 549th Military Police
Company in Fort Amador, Panama
Canal Zone. *Courtesy of the US
Army Military Police Corps
Regimental Museum*

701st Military Police Battalion WLA, with the insignia of the Sixth Army on its windshield, in October 1950. *Courtesy of the US Army Military Police Corps Regimental Museum*

Rear view of the same 701st Military Police Battalion WLA in October 1950. *Courtesy of the US Army Military Police Corps Regimental Museum*

Front-view guide photo for painting a military police WLA, with instructions to paint the body regulation olive drab and paint the lower half of the windscreen, rearview mirror, flasher light, and headlight rim with white enamel, with the "M.P." letters 5 inches high and 4 inches wide in black enamel. *Courtesy of the US Army Military Police Corps Regimental Museum*

Rearview guide photo for painting a military police WLA, with instructions to paint the speedometer case and taillights with white enamel, and to paint the letters "M.P." 2 inches high and 2 inches wide and a 1-inch band on the lower edge of the fender all in white enamel. *Courtesy of the US Army Military Police Corps Regimental Museum*

Side-view guide photo for painting a military police WLA, showing front and rear crash bars painted in white enamel. *Courtesy of the US Army Military Police Corps Regimental Museum*

Side-view guide photo for painting a military police WLA, showing front and rear crash bars painted in white enamel. *Courtesy of the US Army Military Police Corps Regimental Museum*

Fig. 4. CONVENTIONAL WINDSCREEN LETTERING.

4" LETTERS

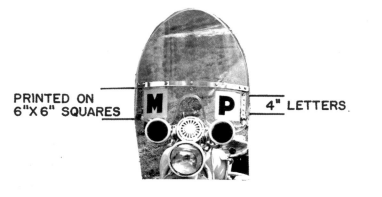

PRINTED ON 6"X 6" SQUARES

4" LETTERS

Fig. 5. LATE MODEL WINDSCREEN LETTERING.

Instructions for painting military police insignia on two types of windscreens. *Courtesy of the US Army Military Police Corps Regimental Museum*

"MILITARY POLICE 2 3/4"(WHITE)

"FT MCP" 3/4"(OD

THIRD ARMY INSIGNIA-"4" LETTER "A"-"2" (RED, WHITE, AND BLUE)

Instructions for painting the front end of a Third Army military police WLA at Fort McPherson, Georgia. *Courtesy of the US Army Military Police Corps Regimental Museum*

Front view of Third Army military police WLA with a conventional windscreen assigned to Camp Gordon, Georgia. *Courtesy of the US Army Military Police Corps Regimental Museum*

Front view of Third Army military police WLA with a late-model windscreen assigned to Camp Gordon, Georgia. *Courtesy of the US Army Military Police Corps Regimental Museum*

Military policeman on a Third Army military police WLA with a late-model windscreen assigned to Camp Gordon, Georgia. *Courtesy of the US Army Military Police Corps Regimental Museum*

WLA of the 307th Military Police Company with another windscreen variation. *Courtesy of the US Army Military Police Corps Regimental Museum*

Front view of military police WLA with US Army license plate number W 610900. *Courtesy of the US Army Military Police Corps Regimental Museum*

Rear view of military police WLA with US Army license plate number W 610900. *Courtesy of the US Army Military Police Corps Regimental Museum*

WLAs and, wearing fiber sun helmets, military policemen of the 772nd Military Police Company, Massachusetts National Guard, a unit that traces its history back to 1638. *Courtesy of the US Army Military Police Corps Regimental Museum*

Notes

Chapter 1: Origins of the WLA

1. Jerry Hatfield, *Inside Harley-Davidson* (Minneapolis: Motorbooks International, 1990), 99, 111, 114, 121.
2. Ibid., 184.
3. David K. Wright, *The Harley-Davidson Motor Company: An Official Ninety-Year History* (Minneapolis: Motorbooks International, 1993), 61.
4. Hatfield, *Inside Harley-Davidson*, 160.
5. Ibid., 180–81.
6. Ibid., 183.
7. Ibid., 190.
8. Harry V. Sucher, *The Iron Redskin: The History of the Indian Motorcycle* (Newbury Park, CA: Haynes, 2010), 242; and Allan Girdler, *The Harley-Davidson and Indian Wars* (Minneapolis: Motorbooks International, 1997), 131.
9. Hatfield, *Inside Harley-Davidson*, 214–15.
10. Ibid., 207.
11. Sucher, *The Iron Redskin*, 247.
12. The most common British military motorcycle was the BSA M20, of which 126,334 were produced. The M20 had a 500 cc engine and four-speed foot shift, girder front forks and no rear suspension, a length of 86 inches and a 54-inch wheelbase, an empty weight of 392 pounds, and 4⅝ inches of ground clearance. The Matchless G3/L had a hydraulically damped telescopic fork, and the Ariel W/NG had a sophisticated girder fork with rebound damping, giving each superior ride comfort on rough roads and off-road. They numbered approximately 52,000 and 40,000, respectively. Triumph and Norton produced 500 cc machines generally similar to the BSA M20 in design.

Chapter 2: Preparing for War

1. Wright, *The Harley-Davidson Motor Company*, 96.
2. According to the official tables of organization and equipment of the Motor Transport Corps of August 1918, the Motor Transport Corps included motorcycle companies whose role was to escort the truck convoys of motor transport companies. *Manual of the Motor Transport Corps*, A.E.F. Headquarters S.O.S. 1919, General Order No. 75, W.D., August 15, 1918 48–54.
3. Information from the US Army Military Police Corps Regimental Museum.
4. Peace Strength Organization Tables, US Marine Corps, for a Reinforced Infantry Brigade & Supplementary Organizations prepared by Division of Operations & Training, War Plans Section, approved 25 Feb 1929, tables No. 17P and 33P (Archives & Special Collections, Library of the Marine Corps, Tables of Organization, Box 1, Bound Volumes 1927, 1929, 1935).
5. Tables of Organization (Peace Strength), US Marine Corps, Marine Brigade, approved 23 August 1939, tables No. 51 and 55 (Archives & Special Collections, Library of the Marine Corps, Tables of Organization, Box 2, Bound Volume 1939).
6. J. J. Hays, *United States Army Ground Forces: Tables of Organization and Equipment; World War II; Field Army and Corps Troops 1940–1945*, vol. 6, *Mechanized Cavalry Regiments, Groups Squadrons and Troops* (Milton Keynes, UK: Military Press 2005), 3.
7. Composite Troop, Fourth Cavalry, Fort Meade, South Dakota, *Report on Experimental Winter Warfare Training for Operation of Cavalry in Snow and Extreme Cold*, April 17, 1941, 15, 33–34 77–78 (Washington, DC: National Archives and Record Administration).

8. Colonel Charles K. Graydon, *With the 101st Cavalry in World War II, 1940–1945*, 9.

Chapter 3: The WLA in the US Army

1. Sucher, *The Iron Redskin*, 244.
2. Armored Division, Table of Organization No. 17, War Department, Washington 29 DC, 15 September 1943; and Yves J. Bellanger, *US Army Armored Division, 1943–1945: Organization, Doctrine, Equipment* (Lexington, KY: Yves J. Bellanger, 2010).
3. Infantry Division—Consolidated Table, Table of Organization No. 7, War Department, Washington, DC, September 1, 1939, 3; and Infantry Division (Square)—Consolidated Table, Table of Organization No. 7, War Department, Washington, DC, November 1, 1940, 2.
4. Infantry Division (Triangular)—Consolidated Table, Table of Organization No. 7-P, War Department, Washington, DC, October 1, 1939, 3.
5. The divisions active in 1939 were the 1st, 2nd, 3rd, 5th, and 6th; the divisions activated in 1940 were the 4th, 7th, 8th, 9th, and 27th. Four of these divisions (the 4th, 6th, 7th, and 8th) began as "Motorized Divisions," a type of unit with fewer men and more motor vehicles, designed for higher mobility. Intended to accompany armored divisions, these units never saw combat as motorized divisions, having been converted to normal infantry divisions with the same numbers by 1943.
6. Infantry Division, Table of Organization No. 7, War Department, Washington, DC, August 1, 1942, 3.
7. Infantry Division, Table of Organization and Equipment No. 7, War Department, Washington 25, DC, July 15, 1943, 3–4; Infantry Division, Table of Organization and Equipment No. 7, War Department, Washington 25, DC, January 24, 1945, 3–4; and Infantry Division, Table of Organization and Equipment No. 7, War Department, Washington 25, DC, June 1, 1945, 2–5.
8. J. J. Hays, *United States Army Ground Forces: Tables of Organization and Equipment; World War II; The Cavalry Divisions; Separate Cavalry Regiments*, vol. 4/I (Milton Keynes, UK: Military Press, 2004), 3–4.
9. Ibid., 6–7.
10. Ibid., 9–10.
11. Ibid., 13–21.
12. Armored Battalion, Regiment, Light, Table of Organization No. 17-15, War Department, Washington, DC, November 18, 1940; and Armored Battalion, Regiment, Medium, Table of Organization No. 17-25, War Department, Washington, DC, November 15, 1940.
13. Armored Battalion, Light, Table of Organization No. 17-15, War Department, Washington, DC, March 1, 1942; and Armored Battalion, Medium, Table of Organization No. 17-25, War Department, Washington, DC, March 1, 1942.
14. Tank Destroyer Battalion, Light, Table of Organization No. 18-15, War Department, Washington, DC, December 24, 1941, 2–3.
15. Tank Destroyer Battalion, Heavy, Table of Organization No. 18-25, War Department, Washington, DC, December 24, 1941, 1–2.
16. Tank Destroyer Battalion, Table of Organization No. 18-25, War Department, Washington, DC, June 8, 1942, 1-2.
17. Light Tank Battalion, Table of Organization and Equipment No. 17-15, War Department, Washington 25, DC, November 12, 1943, 2; Tank Battalion, Table of Organization and Equipment No. 17-25, War Department, Washington 25, DC, September 15, 1943, 2; Light Tank Battalion, Table of Organization and

Equipment No. 17-15, War Department, Washington, DC, November 11, 1944, 2; and Tank Battalion, Table of Organization and Equipment No. 17-25, War Department, Washington 25, DC, November 18, 1944, 2.

18. Tank Destroyer Battalion, Table of Organization No. 18-25, War Department, Washington, DC, January 27, 1943, 1–2; Tank Destroyer Battalion, Self-Propelled, Table of Organization and Equipment No. 18-25, War Department, Washington 25, DC, March 15, 1944, 1–2.

19. Steven J. Zaloga, *US Tank and Tank Destroyer Battalions in the ETO, 1944–45* (Oxford: Osprey, 2005), 34–35.

20. Ibid., 22–92.

21. Ibid., 85–92.

22. Marc W. Miller, *The History of the First Military Police Company in World War II*; Unit History for Month Ending 30 June 1944, F. J. Zaniewski, 1st Lt. Infantry, Unit Historian, Military Police Platoon, 1st Infantry Division; and Reports after Action, from 0001, 1 Oct 1944, to 2400, 31 Oct 1944, Major Raymond R. Regan 1 November 1944, Military Police Regimental Museum.

23. Military Police Company, Army Corps, Table of Organization No 19-37, War Department, Washington, DC, April 1, 1942.

24. Military Police Battalion, Field Army, Table of Organization No 19-35, War Department, Washington, DC, April 1, 1942, 1–2.

25. Military Police Company, Table of Organization No 19-37, War Department, Washington 25, DC, August 19, 1943, 2; and Military Police Battalion, Field Army, Table of Organization No 19-35, War Department, Washington 25, DC, August 19, 1943, 2.

26. Military Police Company, Aviation, Post, Camp, or Station, Table of Organization No 19-217, War Department, Washington, DC, May 1, 1942, 1–2.

27. Military Police Company, Port, Camp, or Station or Military Police Company, Aviation, Table of Organization and Equipment No. 19-217, War Department, Washington 25, DC, January 26, 1945, 3.

28. Military Police Escort Guard Company, Table of Organization 19-47, War Department, Washington, DC, April 1, 1942, 1–2; and Military Police Escort Guard Company, Table of Organization 19-47, War Department, Washington 25, DC, November 25, 1945, 2.

29. Headquarters, 628th Tank Destroyer Battalion, *The History of the 628th Tank Destroyer Bn. in Training and Combat, Prepared by and for the Men Who Saw Action with the Battalion in France,* *Belgium, Luxembourg, Holland and Germany*, 628th Tank Destroyer Battalion. May 9, 1945, www.5ad.org/units/628td. html (accessed July 22, 2012).

30. Bill Wood, "Local Hero," *American Motorcyclist* 52, no. 11 (November 1998): 29–31.

31. Ibid., 31, 46.

Chapter 4: Airborne Division Motorcycles

1. J. J. Hays, *United States Army Ground Forces: Tables of Organization and Equipment; World War II; The Airborne Division, 1942–1945*, vol. 3/I (Milton Keynes, UK: Military Press, 2003), 4.

2. Ibid., 15.

3. J. J. Hays, *United States Army Ground Forces: Tables of Organization and Equipment; World War II; The Airborne Division, 1942–1945*, vol. 3/II (Milton Keynes, UK: Military Press, 2003), 132.

4. Sucher, *The Iron Redskin*, 243.

5. Hays, *United States Army Ground Forces*, vol. 3/I, 4, 7–8, 11–12, 15; and David W. Sullivan, *82nd Airborne Military Police in World War II*, US Army Military Police Corps Museum, February 23, 1984.

Chapter 5: The WLA in the Pacific Theater

1. Marine Corps Table of Organization E-70, Approved 15 April 1943, 2; Marine Corps Table of Organization E-90, Approved 15 April 1943; Marine Corps Table of Organization E-99, Approved 15 April 1943, 2; and Marine Corps Table of Organization E-100, Approved 15 April 1943, 4–6 (Archives & Special Collections, Library of the Marine Corps. Tables of Organization, Box 8).

2. Marine Corps Table of Organization F-100, Approved 5 May 1944 (Archives & Special Collections, Library of the Marine Corps. Tables of Organization, Box 9).

3. Hatfield, *Inside Harley-Davidson*, 120.

4. Hugo Vanneck, "Japan's King of the Road," *Classic Bike*, March 1998: 93–97. Ironically, "Road King" became the name of a Harley-Davidson model half a century later.

Chapter 6: The WLA in the Red Army

1. David Glantz, *Companion to Colossus Reborn: Key Documents and Statistics* (Lawrence: University Press of Kansas, 2005), 157–65.

2. There has been debate on the issue of whether the M72 was the product of reverse engineering of sample BMW R71s acquired through commercial channels or was produced using BMW factory tooling that Germany sent to the Soviet Union under the Molotov-Ribbentrop Pact of 1939. Since the R71 was an obsolete

design and intended for a civilian market that had largely ceased to exist during the war, and the German armed forces were not interested in the R71, it is likely that BMW sent R71 design blueprints and production machinery to the Soviet Union.

3. Hubert P. van Tuyll, *Feeding the Bear: American Aid to the Soviet Union, 1941–1945* (New York: Greenwood, 1989), 156–57.

4. Ibid., 157.

5. Charles W. Sharp, *The Soviet Order of Battle, World War II: An Organizational History of the Major Combat Units of the Soviet Army*, vol. 2, *School of Battle: The Tank Corps and Tank Brigades, January 1942 to 1945* (West Chester, PA: George F. Nafziger, 1995), 52.

6. Glantz, *Companion to Colossus Reborn*, 204–300.

7. Ibid., 270–300.

8. Charles W. Sharp, *The Soviet Order of Battle, World War II: An Organizational History of the Major Combat Units of the Soviet Army*, vol. 3, *Red Storm: Soviet Mechanized Corps and Guards Armored Units 1942 to 1945* (West Chester, PA: George F. Nafziger, 1995), 23–27.

9. Ibid., 93–94.

10. Sharp, *The Soviet Order of Battle*, vol. 2, 49–50.

11. Sharp, *The Soviet Order of Battle*, vol. 3, 24

12. Sharp, *The Soviet Order of Battle*, vol. 2, 52.

13. Defence Intelligence of Ukraine Public Affairs Service, "54th Separate Guards Prut-Pomeranian, Orders of Oleksandr Nevskyi, Bohdan Khmelnytskyi (3rd Class) and Mykhailo Kutuzov (3rd Class) Reconnaissance Battalion," Defence Intelligence, Ministry of Defence of Ukraine, March 18 2014, www.gur.mil.gov.ua/en/content/54-ogrb.html.

Chapter 7: The WLA in Other Allied Armies

1. Sucher, *The Iron Redskin*, 247.

2. For more details about the motorcycles used by the UK armed forces, see Chris Orchard and Steve Madden, *British Forces Motor Cycles, 1925–45* (Gloucestershire, UK: Sutton, 1995), 179–226.

3. Orchard and Madden, *British Forces Motor Cycles, 1925–45*, 198.

4. Ibid., 199.

5. Ibid., 198–99.

6. Ibid.

7. Ibid.

8. Ibid., 199.

9. Ibid., 198–99. Other entities under the British Empire also received the Indian 741B under the same UK contracts. They included Malaya (370), the Indian Admiralty (6), the West Africa Admiralty (4), Trinidad (6), Crown Agents British Honduras (2), Crown Agents Mauritius (16), Crown Agents Ceylon (25), the West African Air Ministry (80), the Middle East Air Ministry (866), Jamaica (5), South Rhodesia (94), and South Caribbean (8). The Belgian Congo received 259.

10. Ibid., 198–99.

11. Charles C. Sharp, *The Soviet Order of Battle, World War II: An Organizational History of the Major Combat Units of the Soviet Army*, vol. 7, *Red Death: Soviet Mountain, Naval, NKVD, and Allied Divisions and Brigades, 1941 to 1945* (West Chester, PA: George F. Nafziger, 1995), 92.

12. Sucher, *The Iron Redskin*, 234.

13. Ibid., 240.

Bibliography

Archives

US Army War College Library and Archives, US Army Heritage & Education Center

Armored Battalion, Regiment, Light, Table of Organization No. 17-15, War Department, Washington, DC, November 18, 1940.

Armored Battalion, Regiment, Medium, Table of Organization No. 17-25, War Department, Washington, DC, November 15, 1940.

Armored Battalion, Light, Table of Organization No. 17-15, War Department, Washington, DC, March 1, 1942.

Armored Battalion, Medium, Table of Organization No. 17-25, War Department, Washington, DC, March 1, 1942.

Armored Division, Table of Organization No. 17, War Department, Washington 29 DC, September 15, 1943.

Infantry Division—Consolidated Table, Table of Organization No. 7, War Department, Washington, DC, September 1, 1939.

Infantry Division (Square)—Consolidated Table, Table of Organization No. 7, War Department, Washington, DC, November 1, 1940.

Infantry Division, Table of Organization No. 7, War Department, Washington, DC, August 1, 1942.

Infantry Division, Table of Organization and Equipment No. 7, War Department, Washington 25, DC, January 24, 1945.

Infantry Division, Table of Organization and Equipment No. 7, War Department, Washington 25, DC, June 1, 1945.

Infantry Division, Table of Organization and Equipment No. 7, War Department, Washington 25, DC, July 15, 1943.

Infantry Division (Triangular)—Consolidated Table, Table of Organization No. 7-P, War Department, Washington, DC, October 1, 1939.

Light Tank Battalion, Table of Organization and Equipment No. 17-15, War Department, Washington, DC, November 11, 1944.

Light Tank Battalion, Table of Organization and Equipment No. 17-15, War Department, Washington 25, DC, November 12, 1943.

Military Police Battalion, Field Army, Table of Organization No. 19-35, War Department, Washington, DC, April 1, 1942.

Military Police Battalion, Field Army, Table of Organization No. 19-35, War Department, Washington 25, DC, August 19, 1943.

Military Police Company, Army Corps, Table of Organization No. 19-37, War Department, Washington, DC, April 1, 1942.

Military Police Company, Aviation, Post, Camp, or Station, Table of Organization No. 19-217, War Department, Washington, DC, May 1, 1942.

Military Police Company, Port, Camp, or Station or Military Police Company, Aviation, Table of Organization and Equipment No. 19-217, War Department, Washington 25, DC, January 26, 1945.

Military Police Company, Table of Organization No. 19-37, War Department, Washington 25, DC, August 19, 1943.

Military Police Escort Guard Company, Table of Organization No. 19-47, War Department, Washington, DC, April 1, 1942.

Military Police Escort Guard Company, Table of Organization No. 19-47, War Department, Washington 25, DC, November 25, 1945.

Tank Battalion, Table of Organization and Equipment No. 17-25, War Department, Washington 25, DC, November 18, 1944.

Tank Battalion, Table of Organization and Equipment No. 17-25, War Department, Washington 25, DC, September 15, 1943.

Tank Destroyer Battalion, Heavy, Table of Organization No. 18-25, War Department, Washington, DC, December 24, 1941.

Tank Destroyer Battalion, Light, Table of Organization No. 18-15, War Department, Washington, DC, December 24, 1941.

Tank Destroyer Battalion, Self-Propelled, Table of Organization and Equipment No. 18-25, War Department, Washington 25, DC, March 15, 1944.

Tank Destroyer Battalion, Table of Organization No. 18-25, War Department, Washington, DC, January 27, 1943.

Tank Destroyer Battalion, Table of Organization No. 18-25, War Department, Washington, DC, June 8, 1942.

US Army Military Police Corps Regimental Museum

Miller, Marc W. *The History of the First Military Police Company in World War II*.

Reports after Action, from 0001, 1 Oct 1944, to 2400, 31 Oct 1944, Major Raymond R. Regan, 1 November 1944, Military Police Regimental Museum.

Sullivan, David W. *82nd Airborne Military Police in World War II*, US Army Military Police Corps Museum, February 23, 1984.

Unit History for Month Ending 30 June 1944, F. J. Zaniewski, 1st Lt. Infantry, Unit Historian, Military Police Platoon, 1st Infantry Division.

US Army Transportation Corps Museum

Manual of the Motor Transport Corps, A.E.F. Headquarters, S.O.S. 1919, General Order No. 75, W.D., August 15, 1918.

National Archives and Records Administration

Composite Troop, Fourth Cavalry, Fort Meade, South Dakota, *Report on Experimental Winter Warfare Training for Operations of Cavalry in Snow and Extreme Cold*, April 17, 1941.

New York State Military Museum

Graydon, Colonel Charles K. *With the 101st Cavalry in World War II, 1940–1945*.

Archives & Special Collections, Library of the Marine Corps

Marine Corps Table of Organization E-70, Approved 15 April 1943, 2; Marine Corps Table of Organization E-90, Approved 15 April 1943; Marine Corps Table of Organization E-99, Approved 15 April 1943, 2; and Marine Corps Table of Organization E-100, Approved 15 April 1943, 4–6 (Archives & Special Collections, Library of the Marine Corps. Tables of Organization, Box 8).

Marine Corps Table of Organization F-100, Approved 5 May 1944 (Archives & Special Collections, Library of the Marine Corps. Tables of Organization, Box 9).

Peace Strength Organization Tables, US Marine Corps, for a Reinforced Infantry Brigade & Supplementary Organizations, prepared by Division of Operations & Training, War Plans Section, approved 25 Feb 1929, tables no. 17P and 33P (Archives & Special Collections, Library of the Marine Corps. Tables of Organization, Box 1, Bound Volumes 1927, 1929, 1935).

Tables of Organization (Peace Strength), US Marine Corps, Marine Brigade, approved 23 August 1939, tables No. 51 and 55 (Archives & Special Collections, Library of the Marine Corps. Tables of Organization, Box 2, Bound Volume 1939).

Published Works

Bellanger, Yves J. *US Army Armored Division, 1943–1945: Organization, Doctrine, Equipment*. Lexington, KY: Yves J. Bellanger, 2010.

Defence Intelligence of Ukraine Public Affairs Service. "54th Separate Guards Prut-Pomeranian, Orders of Oleksandr Nevskyi, Bohdan Khmelnytskyi (3rd Class) and Mykhailo Kutuzov (3rd Class) Reconnaissance Battalion." Defence Intelligence, Ministry of Defence of Ukraine, March 18, 2014. www.gur.mil.gov.ua/en/content/54-ogrb.html.

Girdler, Allan. *The Harley-Davidson and Indian Wars*. Minneapolis: Motorbooks International, 1997.

Glantz, David. *Companion to Colossus Reborn: Key Documents and Statistics*. Lawrence: University Press of Kansas, 2005.

Hatfield, Jerry. *Inside Harley-Davidson*. Minneapolis: Motorbooks International, 1990.

Hays, J. J. *United States Army Ground Forces: Tables of Organization and Equipment; World War II; The Airborne Division, 1942–1945*. Vol. 3/I. Milton Keynes, UK: Military Press, 2003a.

Hays, J. J. *United States Army Ground Forces: Tables of Organization and Equipment; World War II; The Airborne Division, 1942–1945.* Vol. 3/II. Milton Keynes, UK: Military Press, 2003b.

Hays, J. J. *United States Army Ground Forces: Tables of Organization and Equipment; World War II; The Cavalry Divisions; Separate Cavalry Regiments.* Vol. 4/I. Milton Keynes, UK: Military Press, 2004.

Hays, J. J. *United States Army Ground Forces: Tables of Organization and Equipment; World War II; Field Army and Corps Troops, 1940–1945.* Vol. 6, *Mechanized Cavalry Regiments, Groups, Squadrons and Troops.* Milton Keynes, UK: Military Press, 2005.

Headquarters, 628th Tank Destroyer Battalion. *The History of the 628th Tank Destroyer Bn. in Training and Combat, Prepared by and for the Men Who Saw Action with the Battalion in France, Belgium, Luxembourg, Holland and Germany.* 628th Tank Destroyer Battalion, May 9, 1945. www.5ad.org/units/628td.html.

Orchard, Chris, and Steve Madden. *British Forces Motor Cycles, 1925–45.* Gloucestershire, UK: Sutton, 1995.

Sharp, Charles W. *The Soviet Order of Battle, World War II: An Organizational History of the Major Combat Units of the Soviet Army.* Vol. 2, *School of Battle: The Tank Corps and Tank Brigades, January 1942 to 1945.* West Chester, PA: George F. Nafziger, 1995.

Sharp, Charles W. *The Soviet Order of Battle, World War II: An Organizational History of the Major Combat Units of the Soviet Army.* Vol. 3, *Red Storm: Soviet Mechanized Corps and Guards Armored Units, 1942 to 1945.* West Chester, PA: George F. Nafziger, 1995.

Sharp, Charles W. *The Soviet Order of Battle, World War II: An Organizational History of The Major Combat Units of the Soviet Army.* Vol. 7, *Red Death: Soviet Mountain, Naval, NKVD, and Allied Divisions and Brigades, 1941 to 1945.* West Chester, PA: George F. Nafziger, 1995.

Sucher, Harry V. *The Iron Redskin: The History of the Indian Motorcycle.* Newbury Park, CA: Haynes, 2010.

van Tuyll, Hubert P. *Feeding the Bear: American Aid to the Soviet Union, 1941–1945.* New York: Greenwood, 1989.

Vanneck, Hugo. "Japan's King of the Road." *Classic Bike*, March 1998.

Wood, Bill. "Local Hero." *American Motorcyclist* 52, no. 11 (November 1998).

Wright, David K. *The Harley-Davidson Motor Company: An Official Ninety-Year History.* Minneapolis: Motorbooks International, 1993.

Zaloga, Steven J. *US Tank and Tank Destroyer Battalions in the ETO,*